D0593489

For years I have diligently prayed for my husband and my children. Somehow, I just missed praying prayers for me! *Prayers for a Woman's Soul* is my answer to prayer—daily direction in praying for myself so I can become the woman God has created me to be!

—Lynn Cowell, Proverbs 31 speaker and author of
His Revolutionary Love and *Devotions for a Revolutionary Year*

~

As a busy wife, mother, volunteer, and employee, I know in my head the importance of praying for myself. But most days, I'm at the bottom of my prayer list, unless of course there's a problem. But Julie Gillies has inspired me to prioritize praying for myself every day, and in *Prayers for a Woman's Soul* she's made it so easy to do! It's biblical, it's inspiring, and it's practical! It's an invitation to the Source of all peace and joy. I highly recommend this book for any woman needing some inner refreshment.

—Glynnis Whitwer, Proverbs 31 Ministries,
Editor of *P31 Woman* and author of *I Used to Be So Organized*

~

Prayers for a Woman's Soul is like a soothing spa for the harried woman's heart. Julie Gillies bares her own heart in this easy-to-read but meaningful book. Filled with practical Scripture and pointed prayers, each chapter provides refreshment, wisdom, and encouragement for women to reconnect with the Life-Giver so that we're better equipped to give life to others.

—Jody Hedlund, bestselling author of
The Preacher's Bride

With the honesty of a dear friend, Julie Gillies lovingly shares heart stories, painstakingly revealing every woman's deepest need: learning to pray for herself. With 52 topics covering issues from peace to perseverance, Julie invites us to live openly before God, admitting our shortcomings and trusting Him to transform our lives through an intimate prayer relationship.

—Kelly Hancock, founder of FaithfulProvisions.com and author of *Saving Savvy: Smart and Easy Ways to Cut Your Spending in Half and Raise Your Standard of Living…and Giving!*

Prayers for a Woman's Soul is an inspiring, rejuvenating devotional that teaches women not only how to pray for themselves, but how to allow the power of God to speak to their hearts through prayer. Each week, whether using this guide in a group or individually, Julie takes us through prayer topics such as praying for our minds, countenance, and even the distractions that we women face. This book brought clarity to areas in my life that I needed to work on and pray through. You'll find this journey of prayer refreshing to the soul.

—Sandy Coughlin, author of *The Reluctant Entertainer*

Julie Gillies has written a book every woman needs! My heart was fed with encouragement from start to finish. Prayers for a Woman's Soul is the perfect blend of personal stories, powerful prayers, and topic-specific Scriptures to reflect on, helping us draw strength from the Father so we can live from the fullness of all He has for us as women, wives, moms, and friends. I'm going to use it as my personal devotion book this year and get a copy for several friends!

—Renee Swope, bestselling author of *A Confident Heart*, Proverbs 31 Ministries radio co-host and speaker

Prayers
for a
Woman's Soul

Julie K. Gillies

HARVEST HOUSE PUBLISHERS
EUGENE, OREGON

Cover by Koechel Peterson & Associates, Inc., Minneapolis, Minnesota

Cover photo © iStockphoto / Thinkstock

Back cover author photo by Beth McCaa

PRAYERS FOR A WOMAN'S SOUL
Copyright © 2013 by Julie K. Gillies
Published by Harvest House Publishers
Eugene, Oregon 97402
www.harvesthousepublishers.com

ISBN 978-0-7369-4781-7 (pbk.)
ISBN 978-0-7369-4782-4 (eBook)

Printed in China

13 14 15 16 17 18 19 20 21 / RDS-CD / 10 9 8 7 6 5 4 3 2

Acknowledgments

"For a dream comes with much business and painful effort."

—Ecclesiastes 5:3 AMP

To my husband, Keith, for believing in me and not allowing me to quit, eating cold cereal for dinner without complaint, and for buying me an author nameplate before my first article sold. You're the best encourager ever.

To my precious daughter, Emily, for leaving my office doors closed (most mornings) so I could meet my daily word quota and for predicting years ago, through a hand-colored page, that mom would publish a book. I love you to pieces.

To Angela Jimenez, Courtney Moore, Diane Lafler, Rhoda Wilhoit, Bethany Hostetler, Krista King, Kathy Mast, Deborah Gallicchio, and Noelle Yoder, for reading my first three chapters, offering honest feedback, and praying. You helped shape this book. Thanks for walking out the beginning of the dream with me.

To the precious women who prayed for me as I wrote—you know who you are. Thank you, thank you. May God's reward officially rock your world.

And to the Lord, who unearths buried dreams, brushes them off, and hands them back to us. Your power truly works best in weakness.

Contents

My Mind 15

My God Hears Me 20

My Attitude 24

My Willingness to Forgive 29

My Fear 34

My Distractions 39

My Hope 44

My Countenance 49

My Meekness 53

My Dreams 58

My Joy 63

My Humility 67

My Love 71

My Physical Health 76

My Wisdom 81

My Emotions 86

My Past 91

My Peace 95

My Value 100

God's Timing in My Life 104

My Mouth. 109

My Thoughts 114

My Identity 118

My Walk with God 122

My Ability to Hear God's Voice 126

My Balance 130

My Weariness 134

My Perseverance 139

My Worship 143

My Strength 147

My Decisions 151

My Expectations 156

My Disqualified Feelings 160

My Security. 165

My Guilt. 169

My Focus 173

My Plans 178

My Contentment 183

My Determination 188

My Self-Control. 192

My Tension-Filled Life 196

My Comparison Issues 201

My Obedience. 206

My Desire to Be Noticed 210

My Patience 215

My Trust in God 220

My Confidence 224

My Perfectionism 229

My Marriage. 234

My Calling 239

My Love for Scripture 244

My God-Given Destiny. 249

Introduction

"Be joyful in hope, patient in affliction, faithful in prayer."

—Romans 12:12

I settled into seat 10-A, flipped open a magazine, and unwrapped a piece of chocolate. My annual October flight from Florida to Michigan started out like any other. In a few hours I would arrive at my sister's house in a charming small town and our indulgent girlfriend weekend would begin. Facials, mani-pedis, high tea, and afternoon naps beckoned.

This time, however, as the flight attendant began speaking, I felt the God-nudge. You know, the one that compels you to stop what you're doing and pay attention. I looked up from the article I'd been skimming and listened intently to the woman in the navy blazer.

"In the event of the loss of cabin pressure, oxygen masks will descend." The petite brunette stood at the front of our cabin, demonstrating how to attach a small, yellow, Tupperware-type bowl over her nose and mouth with an elastic band. "Place the mask on yourself first, and then help those around you."

I shook my head. *Hmmm. I would have automatically slapped those masks on my kids first.*

Suddenly, God spoke. *You need to begin to pray for yourself. Regularly.*

I shook my head. *Really?*

As the plane ascended over Tampa, I thought about all of the people and situations for which I regularly prayed: my husband, children, and grandchildren, daughter-in-law, friends, our neighborhood situations, church issues, the military, world events…the list went on. But when I thought about it, I realized there was no time set apart for me to just pray for *me*. It actually never occurred to me to pray for myself on a regular basis. I was in the habit of placing the oxygen mask on those around me first, and in so doing, neglecting my own lifeline.

That was about to change.

And God knew it was a change I desperately needed. My marriage was sinking like a brick in the Gulf of Mexico. I struggled to balance women's ministry obligations and homeschooling, but most days I felt like I was about thirty seconds away from total collapse.

As women we are nurturers and caretakers. We're wives, mothers, friends, sisters, and daughters who work at home or hurry out to get to the office. We homeschool or we help with homework. Our lives are busy, full. We give out until there is nothing left.

We're front-burner prayer women, praying for whatever is boiling over at that moment (and there's always something boiling over!). We can't afford *not* to cover ourselves with prayer on a regular basis. Like an oxygen mask in an airplane cabin that's lost its pressure, praying for ourselves fortifies and equips us so we can soar.

When the Holy Spirit spoke to me that day on the airplane, it was as if I'd been handed vanilla-scented oxygen and a free trip to a luxury spa, all at once. I began to understand that regularly praying for myself would somehow begin to change me...and maybe even my circumstances.

Initially the *only* uninterrupted time I could find to pray for myself was in the shower, so that's where I started. That was many years ago, and it's still how I begin my day: immersed in prayer and effectively equipped by God.

Praying for myself has enabled me to persevere when I wanted to quit, to forgive when I wanted to hold a grudge, to hope when reality screamed "Impossible!" and to remain close to God when I ached so badly I wanted to run and never look back. In essence, praying for myself not only helped me, it transformed me.

This is not a suggestion to neglect praying for others, or to pray exclusively (and selfishly) for ourselves only. It's the recognition that if Jesus needed to pray for Himself, then so should we. It's the humble acknowledgement that we cannot give away what we do not have; that we need a divine download of peace, joy, forgiveness, wisdom, and strength to get through our day. Praying for ourselves is not selfish—it's absolutely necessary. Scripture says we have not because we ask not (James 4:2). So let's ask God to refresh and infuse us with life-giving strength through prayer for ourselves every day.

Step out in expectation; stir up your faith and ask God to meet you as you make time to regularly pray for yourself. Take time to breathe in—and truly take to heart—the personalized Scriptures. Though not rewriting Scripture, these verses appear in a fresh, new light, and will help you see God's word in a surprisingly intimate way—straight from God's heart to yours. You may just find that meditating on Scriptures is much more meaningful when they're personalized. So relax, grab a hot beverage, get comfy, and prepare to soak…in extravagant prayer.

My Mind

Confession: For years I walked around with a destructive, negative, and critical mindset without recognizing it. Raised in a tumultuous home that simmered with anger, fear, and resentment, I picked up these deadly thought processes that grew like kudzu over my mind and threatened to choke out every positive thought.

Years later, enduring a miserable marriage, I regularly cried myself to sleep, still unaware that negative mindsets poisoned my thoughts. I'd wake up in the morning and rehash my husband's harsh words of the night before, tell myself that things were never going to change, and give in to every negative, critical thought that happened to float by the rest of the day. I was miserable.

It wasn't until a time of prayer at a weekend women's retreat that I suddenly became aware of my critical mindset. Even so, over the following years it remained a real effort not to give in to the negative thoughts I had regularly entertained most of my life. It took time and concerted effort, but as I prayed and spent time reading my Bible, wrong mindsets were replaced with healthy, godly thoughts.

You may not fight a negative or critical attitude like I did. Maybe worry, fear, or insecurity bombard your mind regularly. That's the enemy's plan: to consistently assault our minds until we surrender.

We must fight him every step of the way. As busy women, we don't have one brain cell to spare. And as godly women, we cannot yield any mind-turf to the enemy. The first goal when praying for our minds is the ability to recognize when we're under attack. God's word tell us, "Submit yourselves, then, to God. Resist the devil, and he will flee from you" (James 4:7).

The number-one way to resist the enemy is through prayer. Though the attacks against our mind can be subtle, God grants discernment when we ask Him. He will reveal to us what we are not always capable of discerning apart from the Holy Spirit: erroneous, potentially destructive thoughts and mindsets. Whether the intrusions in our minds are vestiges from the distant past or yesterday's hurts and disappointments, we can face every day with clear minds and godly mindsets.

Daily Prayer

Father,

Thank You for the blood of Jesus, which cleanses my mind. Give me a sharp, clear mind and enable me to grasp and understand the truth of Your word, which has power to transform my mind. Where I unknowingly possess wrong mindsets, please change them and give me a healthy, accurate mind. Where the enemy has made inroads in my mind, I ask You to make me aware and help me to cooperate with the workings of Your Holy Spirit. Repave those paths and bring freedom to every area of my mind.

Grant me discernment to recognize when my mind is being attacked by the enemy. Enable me to stand against the schemes of the enemy and the daily bombardments that come against my mind. Thank You for freedom from every wrong mindset, including: *(List thoughts and mindsets from which you desire freedom).*

Equip my mind with Your helmet of salvation. Protect my mind from every evil influence. I submit my mind to You and thank You for granting me ever-increasing discernment, wisdom, and an understanding mind. Thank You that I have the mind of Christ, and I hold the thoughts, feelings and purposes of His heart. Renew my mind and grant me a fresh mental and spiritual attitude. In Jesus's wonderful name, amen.

God's Word for Me

I will not conform to the pattern of this world, but will be transformed by the renewing of my mind (Romans 12:2).

For God has not given me a spirit of timidity (of cowardice, of craven and cringing and fawning fear), but [He has given me a spirit] of power and of love and of calm and of well-balanced mind and of discipline and self-control
(2 Timothy 1:7 AMP).

I have the mind of Christ (1 Corinthians 2:16).

The LORD listens to my cry and will give me the discerning mind he promised
(Psalm 119:169 NLT).

My heart is at peace, and it gives life to my body
(Proverbs 14:30).

I have a wise mind and wise speech, My words are
wise and persuasive (Proverbs 16:23 AMP).

The Holy Spirit controls my mind, which leads to
life and peace (Romans 8:6 NLT).

My God Hears Me

I sat in the front seat of my car and stared out into the night. My breathing, no longer jagged and desperate, began to come in regular, calm intervals. Tears still trickled, their deluge slowed from exhaustion. I closed my eyes and whispered, *God, I need You. I can't keep doing this. Help me.*

I held my breath, anticipating a burst of radiant light through the windshield accompanied by the Hallelujah chorus, half a legion of angels, and God's audible voice. I waited, my body tense in anticipation, my ears straining to hear. I wanted to believe that God heard my desperate cries and would show up any second in a dramatic, parting of the seas sort of way. But none of those things happened. Instead, in the deep corners of my heart, a tiny ripple of peace fluttered in. And though it wasn't what I hoped for or expected, it was enough.

I backed out of the park's gravel driveway and began the drive home, determined to face my miserable marriage with God's help. I had so longed to hear His voice in a powerful way. What I didn't understand was that the boiling turmoil in my soul prevented me from discerning His presence, and that it is Him who always hears me, not the other way around.

There are seasons in our lives when God's words jump at us, making their presence known in spite of our busyness and our distractions. But we endure seasons of silence as well, when in spite of our most sincere efforts we hear nothing but the echoes of our own desperate longings.

But God is not like us—He has no problem hearing us. In fact, He *always* hears us. When Jesus said, "Father, I thank you that you have heard me…you always hear me…" (John 11:41-42) He said it aloud *for our benefit*. Our Savior longs for us to understand this simple yet profound truth: God always listens and hears, just like the mother of a newborn strains to hear her baby's first waking noises. That means that He hears our softest whimper; He listens when others lose interest or are unavailable. Always.

I take immense comfort in that.

Jesus's thrilling words declare what my soul now knows to be true: God is deeply interested in what we have to say and hears every word we utter, even when it doesn't feel like He's heard us. Even when we're tempted to believe He is not listening. It is with this amazing truth that we arm ourselves: God *is* always listening, and He *always* hears us.

Daily Prayer

Dear Lord,

My heart longs to believe that You are always listening and that You always hear me. Help me truly believe Your word and allow this wonderful truth to sink deep into the farthest corners of my heart. God, I know that I can believe Your word because You are faithful and utterly trustworthy. Thank You for loving me enough to listen to me. You are crazy about me, and as Your daughter, You desire to hear me, spend time with me, and listen to the cries of my heart. Thank You, Lord, that even though You are the Creator of the universe, You listen. You hear—because I am that important and valuable to You.

Lord, when I'm tempted to think that You have not heard me because the answer hasn't come or perhaps it's not the answer I desire, help me to trust Your heart. Help me to whisper to myself with confidence, like the Psalmist, "The Lord listens and heeds when I call to Him." In Jesus's name, amen.

God's Word for Me

I know that the LORD has set me apart for himself;
the LORD hears when I call to him
(Psalm 4:3).

In the morning, LORD, you hear my voice; in the
morning I lay my requests before you and wait
expectantly (Psalm 5:3).

The LORD has heard my cry for mercy;
the LORD accepts my prayer
(Psalm 6:9).

In my distress I called to the LORD; I cried to my
God for help. From his temple he heard my voice;
my cry came before him, into his ears
(Psalm 18:6).

Praise be to the LORD, for he has heard my cry
for mercy (Psalm 28:6).

In my alarm I said, "I am cut off from your sight!"
Yet you heard my cry for mercy when I called
to you for help (Psalm 31:22).

The LORD hears the needy and does not despise
his captive people (Psalm 69:33).

My Attitude

It was supposed to be a relaxing trip to the beach. But when four grandkids under the age of seven come along, even the most pristine surroundings can leave you feeling far from rested. Somehow the children's exuberance, coupled with our rogue umbrella, unexpectedly rough waves, and skydiving seagulls bent on stealing our sandwiches made it far from peaceful, even with my daughter-in-law and teen daughter's help.

Hours later we arrived home, a sweaty, exhausted bunch with most of the beach lodged in our swimsuits. When I stepped into our kitchen, my foot swung forward—but my shoe stayed glued to the floor. *Hmmmm. Now that's strange.* Slipping my foot out of my sandal, I followed a sticky, shimmering trail to the cupboard under the kitchen sink and let out a groan. The entire contents of a large jar of super-sticky homemade ant poison syrup had spilled, coating everything under the sink with half an inch of goop and dripping out onto the kitchen floor like a gooey, slow-motion waterfall.

I was hobbling with one shoe toward the laundry room to grab the mop when I noticed a disgusting yellowish blob on the living room carpet. "Mom, the dog threw up!" my daughter announced, making my shoulders kink. "And there's some in the family room too!"

I wish I could tell you that I calmly cleaned up all the messes that day (including the sand in my swimsuit) with a good attitude and a dash of humor. But the truth is my attitude was far less pleasant than the stuff left on my carpet by our Australian shepherd. Though I didn't scream at anyone outwardly, the mess on my inside far exceeded the mess in my house.

Finally, after a shower, a late lunch, and cleaning up all the goop and dog puke, I felt much better. But I knew my attitude needed to change. God showed me that day what it took to push me over the edge. And I knew I needed to pray.

Our bad attitudes have the ability to spread and infiltrate every square inch of our home and family, much like the syrupy ant poison that leaked out of my cupboards. Here's the good news: We can clean up a bad attitude fast. All we need is the ability to recognize our bad attitude, the willingness to accept responsibility, and a heart that is quick to repent.

God is able to help us see our attitudes as they

really are, grant us readiness to accept responsibility, and then give us hearts to make things right.

Daily Prayer

Dear Lord,

Please forgive me for every wrong attitude I've demonstrated this week. I want to recognize when my attitude is wrong, accept responsibility for a bad attitude, and quickly repent of every sinful attitude. I submit my attitude to You, Lord. I pray that the words of my mouth and the meditation of my heart will be pleasing to You, God, and that can only happen if You cleanse my heart and grant me grace.

Help me not to allow myself to be negative, critical, sarcastic, or judgmental. Help me not to think of myself as better than others or to think of myself more highly than I ought to. Enable me not to harbor resentment or any other sinful attitude.

Show me when I veer off course and unknowingly slip into a wrong attitude. Keep my heart tender and sensitive toward You. Help me to be quick to apologize to my spouse, children, and others when I've displayed an inappropriate attitude so that my heart will be clean before You.

Lord, grant me a fresh mental and spiritual attitude. Help me demonstrate and model a consistently godly attitude before my family and others. I pray that I will walk in the Spirit and not in the flesh, and that my attitude will always be pleasing to You. Grant me a willing heart to sustain me, Lord. In the precious name of Jesus, amen.

God's Word for Me

I will be made new in the attitude of my mind
(Ephesians 4:23).

May these words of my mouth and this meditation of my heart be pleasing in your sight, LORD, my Rock and my Redeemer
(Psalm 19:14).

Create in me a pure heart, O God,
and renew a steadfast spirit within me
(Psalm 51:10).

I will have the same attitude that
Christ Jesus had (Philippians 2:5 NLT).

I will clothe myself with humility
(1 Peter 5:5).

I will do my best to present myself to God as
one approved, a worker who does not need to be
ashamed and who correctly handles the word of
truth (2 Timothy 2:15).

I will do everything without grumbling or
arguing (Philippians 2:14).

My Willingness to Forgive

While attending a party many years ago, an acquaintance made unkind statements that shocked me. Rattled, I left the gathering early, rehearsing our conversation on the drive home. *Did she really say that? Did I misunderstand?* By the time I walked in my front door half an hour later, I was not happy. In fact, I was flat-out angry. I stomped straight into the bathroom and began giving my teeth a severe brushing.

When my husband innocently wandered into the bathroom to ask how my evening had been, he hardly expected my irate, toothpaste-flinging response. Ducking for cover, the look in his eyes told me I needed to simmer down and pray—fast.

I allowed myself a few days to calm down, pray, and really think about what had happened. When I felt my attitude was finally right, I made what I hoped would be a conciliatory phone call to the person involved. Unfortunately, as sometimes happens, the issue remained unresolved. I wanted to make things right, but in this situation it simply wasn't possible. I felt trapped.

Romans 12:18 says, "If it is possible, as far as it depends on you, live at peace with everyone." But what about when it's not possible? What then?

As I prayed about the situation, God clearly showed me a picture of a large, jaw-shaped bear trap made of jagged metal. Then He told me that the purpose of a dangerous bear trap is twofold: to inflict injury and to prevent the animal from moving forward.

Clearly I had two options that day. I could either step into the bear trap, injuring and trapping myself in the process, or cut a wide swath around it, bypassing it altogether.

In the heat of the moment, it's easy to zero in on the pain of a misunderstanding, harsh words, or an ugly reaction. Our emotions become inflamed and it feels nearly impossible to move forward. But unforgiveness can turn into the spiritual equivalent of a bear trap clamped around our leg. We must choose to forgive even the unresolved issues (ouch!) or the trap will remain embedded in our flesh and the enemy will succeed in chaining us to that painful place.

I truly forgave my friend that day, even though it wasn't easy. Forgiveness does not require the other party to participate; it's a choice we make to release them and willingly let go of our anger and resentment.

Though it's not always possible to navigate around

the bear traps the enemy hides in our lives, how quickly we're released is *always* our choice. When we make the decision to forgive, the bear trap's spring is released and God's healing and grace rushes into the situation and into our hearts.

Daily Prayer

Father God,

It's so easy for me to get caught up in the heat of an ugly moment. But I desire to always walk in forgiveness in every situation—even unresolved situations. Please grant me a willing heart, and help me choose to forgive even when it feels especially hard. Your word says I must forgive others or You will not forgive me, so right now I determine in my heart that I will choose to walk in forgiveness. Help me when my emotions flare up, God. Help me to see that forgiveness is truly a choice—a decision I make and not a feeling. And help me continually choose as an act of my will to walk in forgiveness every day. I understand that so much of the time the hurt or offense was not only unintentional, but the person involved is unaware of the pain they've caused me. Help me to remember this and be quick to forgive and let it go.

I also desire to walk forward in freedom, Lord, not unforgiveness, even when others willingly choose to hurt me. I will not allow resentment or bitterness to grow in my heart. I desire to be free from any and all unforgiveness lurking in my heart. So right now, I choose to forgive the following people: *(Write a list of the people who come to mind. After you've prayerfully forgiven each one, destroy the paper.)* Thank You for giving me Your grace and enabling me to continually choose to forgive. In the precious name of Jesus, amen.

God's Word for Me

For if I forgive other people when they sin against me, my heavenly Father will also forgive me (Matthew 6:14).

Who can discern their own errors? Forgive my hidden faults (Psalm 19:12).

I will forgive my brother or sister who sins against me not seven times, but seventy times seven times (Matthew 18:21–22).

Forgive me my sins, for I also forgive everyone who sins against me (Luke 11:4).

And when I stand praying, if I hold anything against anyone, I will forgive them, so that my Father in heaven may forgive me my sins (Mark 11:25).

Even if someone sins against me seven times in a day and seven times comes back to me saying "I repent," I will forgive them (Luke 17:4).

But with you there is forgiveness (Psalm 130:4).

My Fear

Like my freckles and blue eyes, fear was an integral part of me. Steeped in fear at a young age, my perspective was skewed, but I had no other frame of reference to understand that it was abnormal. Though I didn't like or quite understand it, fear and I were inseparable.

I learned at a tender age not to make my dad angry, and how to get out of the way, fast, when my parents got into a shouting match or when my dad lost his temper. But what I didn't learn until later—much later—is that fear completely saturated and controlled me. The residue of fear clung to me like mildew on a fountain ledge. It simply would not let go.

Years later I married a good man who had himself been deeply wounded by his dad. His frequent tirades made every cell in my body quiver. Our home simmered with tension.

I hated it.

Then I met Jesus. Eventually, my husband did too. And though it took time, fear eventually lost its grip, one white-knuckled finger at a time. The more I got to know the Lover of my soul, the more fear was displaced. As I clung to Jesus, fear became diluted by a force more powerful than any other: God's love.

Recently, while visiting in North Carolina, I noticed something strange. A brand new door stood at the front of a brand new building, but it lacked a doorknob of any kind. Boldly painted across it were the following words: "This door is permanently locked and blocked."

My initial reaction was, *How ridiculous is that? Who would put a door at the front of a brand new building, then lock it—and announce to the world that it's permanently blocked?* It just seemed like a waste.

But then I realized that the words on that crazy door mirror the words on the door of my heart. The words that God Himself has written because the door of fear had been closed, blocked, and permanently sealed in my life. And it happened one prayer at a time. As I delved into God's Word and believed it, applied it, prayed it, and walked it out, the fear disappeared.

Whether the fear in your life manifests itself as worry, doubt, insecurity, or timidity (or anything else!), know this: Jesus is in the door-closing business. Because even though the wrong door may have been opened in our lives, God wants to permanently block it so that the enemy can no longer gain access to that area of our lives.

Once those wrong doors are closed, we will live fearless lives. Then, just like the door I saw, people will clearly see that fear cannot enter. And that will be a clear sign of God's amazing work on the door of our hearts.

Daily Prayer

Dear Lord,

I confess that there are times when I am especially fearful, yet I know it is not Your will for me to walk in fear. I believe and declare that You are greater than all my fears. Thank You for Your Holy Spirit, who strengthens me and enables me to be brave, even when I feel afraid.

Show me any roots of unresolved fear from my past. Bring healing and courage, and strengthen my heart so that I will not fear. When fear comes upon me, help me to combat it through prayer and reading Your word. Help me not to allow myself to be frightened or to make decisions based on fear. I resolve, by Your grace, not to walk in fear. I will choose not to allow myself to be frightened and intimidated, God, because I know that You are always with me. Because

I am Your daughter, I will not allow fear to have power over me.

God, when I feel afraid, I will choose to trust in You. Grant me courage, boldness, and peace in every situation. Give me a heart that is continually strengthened and assured by Your mighty power. Father God, I ask You to permanently lock and block every open door of fear in my life. In the mighty name of Jesus, amen.

God's Word for Me

I will wait for the LORD; I will be strong and take heart and wait for the LORD (Psalm 27:14).

When I am afraid, I put my trust in you (Psalm 56:3).

You are my refuge and my shield; I have put my hope in your word (Psalm 119:114).

I will be strong and courageous. I will not be afraid; I will not be discouraged, for the LORD my God will be with me wherever I go (Joshua 1:9).

I will not fear, though the earth give way and the mountains fall into the heart of the sea (Psalm 46:2).

I will not be afraid, for you are with me (Isaiah 43:5).

I will be strong and take heart because I hope in the Lord (Psalm 31:24).

My Distractions

Remember Martha? She lived a distracted life, and she didn't even have Facebook. In fact, Martha had Jesus Himself right there in her house—yet she busied herself to distraction.

Two thousand years later, one of women's primary conflicts is *still* distractions, only they have multiplied far beyond what Martha ever imagined. On the average day, most of us e-mail, Google, tweet, blog, Facebook, text, and leave a voicemail (or two). Headline News beams live events into our living rooms, satellite radio gives us nonstop talk, and call-waiting interrupts our phone conversations. We juggle our church commitments, meetings, friendships, chores, and errands. We taxi our kids to various sports events, lessons, and birthday parties. And if we work outside the home, we manage to do many of these things after putting in eight hours on the job.

As a homeschooling mom who also works from home, distractions can be lethal to my productivity. I confess that in spite of my best efforts, one single distraction invariably leads to another, and before I know it I'm completely off course. Worse, distractions seem to eliminate two crucial elements that I desperately need: brain cells and focus.

Here's the good news: God knew that the world we live in would eventually overflow with an abundance of knowledge, information, and activity. He knew we would be alive right now (see Acts 17:26) and face the distractions that technology and our culture offer. I believe God wants us to know that we are not alone in this conflict. Immanuel, God with us, is here to help us weigh our options and, hopefully, choose wisely.

The truth is, like Martha, each one of us has the capacity to be overly busy with many things. Though we are seemingly pulled in hundreds of directions in just a single day, we would do well to remember that we have need of one thing: keeping Jesus at the center of all we do.

It's nearly impossible not to be at least occasionally distracted. As women, wives, and mothers, we're the busiest people on the planet. However, with Christ all things are possible. He alone can grant us the clarity and wisdom to make wise choices so that we recognize and avoid needless distractions. By the power of His Holy Spirit, our focus really can be on the One thing we have need of: Jesus.

Daily Prayer

Father God,

I am tugged in so many directions. Grant me the ability to focus on You first, then the tasks You've given me, regardless of the distractions coming my way. When I'm overly busy, show me. Help me to recognize and resist distractions that are not from You. Enable me to prioritize and be led by Your Spirit. Help me to realize the difference between distractions and the need to shift gears temporarily, Lord, because I know that sometimes what I perceive as an interruption or distraction is an opportunity from You.

Enable me to walk in self-discipline against regular time-wasting activities and grow in self-control in each area that You show me. Give me the ability to resist flitting from thing to thing without accomplishing much. Enable me to remain focused on You as Jesus was focused on You—He only did what He saw You doing. Lord, show me what I am to do, and help me to walk gracefully away from everything else. Cause my thoughts to become agreeable to Your will, and then my plans will be established and succeed.

Help me, Lord, to keep the main thing (Jesus) the main thing. Today and every day. In the wonderful name of Jesus, amen.

God's Word for Me

I will commit to the Lord whatever I do, and he will establish my plans (Proverbs 16:3).

I will look away [from all that distracts] to Jesus, my leader and the source of my faith (Hebrews 12:2 AMP).

I wait for the Lord more than watchmen wait for the morning, more than watchmen wait for the morning (Psalm 130:6).

I lift up my eyes to the mountains—where does my help come from? My help comes from the Lord, the Maker of heaven and earth (Psalm 121:1-2).

I will not allow the worries of this life, the deceitfulness of wealth and the desires for other things to come in and choke the word (Mark 4:19).

I will devote my heart and soul to seeking the
LORD my God (1 Chronicles 22:19).

Many are the plans in my heart, but it is the
LORD's purpose for me that will stand
(Proverbs 19:21 AMP).

My Hope

Eleven years is a long time to pray a specific prayer without an answer, especially when it involves your husband's salvation. It's a long time to maintain faith that the One who hears all prayers has heard yours. It's a long time to hold on to hope. And frankly, hopelessness had begun to relentlessly bombard my heart.

So God spoke to me through a dream. In my dream, a beautiful wooden hope chest rested at the foot of my bed. In the middle of the night, a thief broke in through my bedroom window, tiptoed to my hope chest, and silently lifted the lid. He stole everything I'd stored up for my future, leaving my hope chest completely empty.

When I awoke, the Spirit of the Lord told me that Satan was stealing my hope; the enemy wanted to leave me without hope that my husband would ever turn to God. John 10:10 says, "The thief comes only to steal and kill and destroy."

After this dream, I realized that hope is something that we must make a diligent effort to hold on to. Hope is a provision from the Lord that will keep us going when our circumstances tempt us to feel, well, hopeless. Hope keeps our dreams alive. Hebrews 6:19 calls hope an "anchor for the soul, firm and secure." It prevents us from drifting into the sea of despair.

Satan uses the negative circumstances in our lives to try to steal our hope. When things look really, really bad for us, we would do well to remember Abraham. Romans 4:18 says, "Against all hope, Abraham in hope believed and so became the father of many nations." Abraham was an old man. Verse 19 tells us that his body was "as good as dead." Abraham faced the facts yet refused to give up hope.

Are you looking at a situation that seems absolutely hopeless? I'm convinced God doesn't mind when we look at our situations and realize that the facts *seem* hopeless. We can't pretend away our circumstances. However, we mustn't allow the situation to sway our belief in God's ability. We can magnify the power and the ability of the Lord to do that which is seemingly impossible in our situation. We can face the facts, yet refuse to give up our hope!

Whatever we are walking through, God wants us to hold on to hope. His hand is not too short. He is at work in spite of how awful things might look. So take courage; stand firm and hold fast. We can dare to dream the dreams and hope for the things that God has tenderly placed inside our hope chests.

Daily Prayer

Dear Lord,

In my human frailty, I sometimes perceive events, circumstances, or issues in my life as utterly hopeless. Sometimes it feels as though things will never change, and I'm tempted to just give up on the inside. But right now I am placing every feeling of hopelessness at Your feet, and I'm asking You to fill me to the brim with Your unwavering hope. Flood my heart with hope and the revelation that You alone are my hope and my strength.

Please help me not to allow the enemy to steal my hope. Help me to guard it—to protect it vigilantly. Allow me to clearly perceive when Satan moves in and my hope begins to wane, so I can resist him at the onset. I resolve to resist the enemy's attempts to make me feel hopeless. Help me to become a prisoner of hope to You, oh God. I know the dreams and the plans You have for me are good. Right now I

determine to believe Your word, believe the promises
You have given me, and believe that You are greater
than every circumstance in my life that tempts me to
feel hopeless. I place every situation, every life event,
and every secret longing of my heart into Your tender,
capable hands, Lord. Enable me to hold tightly to the
precious gift of hope You've entrusted to me. In the
powerful name of Jesus I pray, amen.

God's Word for Me

Why, my soul, are you downcast? Why so dis-
turbed within me? Put your hope in God, for
I will yet praise him, my Savior and my God
(Psalm 42:5).

The Lord is my inheritance; therefore I will hope
in him (Lamentations 3:24 NLT).

And hope does not put me to shame, because
God's love has been poured out into my heart
through the Holy Spirit (Romans 5:5).

I hope for what I do not yet have; I wait for it patiently (Romans 8:25).

Lord, my hope is in you (Psalm 39:7).

Therefore my heart is glad and my tongue rejoices; my body also will rest in hope (Acts 2:26).

For you have been my hope, Sovereign LORD, my confidence since my youth (Psalm 71:5).

My Countenance

*D*o *I walk around with a pinched look on my face?* My self-examination revealed a truth I wasn't exactly sure I wanted to know, but in the end couldn't deny. I wore stress (and a myriad of other not-so-pleasant emotions) across my face like a tight, scary mask. My kids were witnesses. So was my husband. And now, as I stared at the video, I saw it too.

That day marked the beginning of my acute awareness of how strongly my countenance affects my family and those around me. If communication is 90 percent body language, my countenance screamed so loudly it's unlikely my words were actually heard.

Initially I had no idea how to go about changing things. I just knew that I wanted to change. I wanted to look happy. Heck, I wanted to *be* happy. That's when I realized that my countenance is a reflection of what's going on deep within the hinterlands of my heart. A lot of the time, I was out of touch with what my heart felt, and simply barreling through the day in my attempt to Get Things Done. But my countenance always let those around me know. Eventually, I caught on.

The only real way for authentic countenance change is to spend time with the One who can make His countenance shine on us. As time passes, we begin to take on the characteristics of the One who changes not only our faces, but our hearts. Because that's where it all starts.

In Psalm 42:5, King David asks, "Why, my soul, are you downcast? Why so disturbed within me?" I don't know whether David caught a glimpse of his reflection in the watering pond, but he recognized that his countenance was off, and he knew something needed to change.

I dare you to ask your spouse, your closest friend, and God Himself whether or not you walk around with a pinched, stressed, or unhappy look on your face. Make a list of a few close friends or family members you can ask.

Being aware of our need for a countenance change is a necessary first step. Crying out to God for radical, permanent change and spending time in His presence will bring the transformation for which we yearn. Psalm 42:5 goes on to say, "Put your hope in God, for I will yet praise him, my Savior and my God."

With self-awareness and God's help, our faces, hearts, and eventually our countenance can be drastically altered.

Daily Prayer

Father God,

Forgive me for allowing myself to display a cranky, irritated, or dark countenance. I long for my countenance to be an accurate reflection of You—Your love, faithfulness, and goodness. Yet so many times I allow the issues, disappointments, and trials of my day to form a cloud over my heart—and my face.

Change my countenance, Lord. As I focus on You and spend time reading Your word I believe You will change my outward appearance by changing the things that are unseen—my heart—and the deep things inside me I cannot even name. Lord, go to those places—I give You the key right now—and I ask You to go where I haven't previously allowed You to go. Please bring healing, freedom, and fresh, new light so that my countenance will be transformed.

Only You can change my countenance, Lord. Help me to remember to keep my focus on You, Jesus. It's when I'm looking at You that I can most accurately reflect Your image, and that's what I long to do. In the precious name of Jesus, amen.

God's Word for Me

I have a happy heart which makes my face
cheerful (Proverbs 15:13).

The LORD lifts up his [approving] countenance
upon me and gives me peace (Numbers 6:26 AMP).

I will put my hope in God, for I will yet praise
him, my Savior and my God (Psalm 42:11).

As iron sharpens iron, so one person sharpens
another (Proverbs 27:17).

Lift up the light of your countenance upon me,
O Lord (Psalm 4:6 AMP).

Wisdom brightens my face and changes its hard
appearance (Ecclesiastes 8:1).

But you, LORD, are a shield around me, my glory,
the One who lifts my head high (Psalm 3:3).

My Meekness

I sat at a red light in rush-hour traffic, hyperventilating. The business man in the gleaming white sedan in front of me had abruptly cut me off. Behind me, a teenage girl with pink streaks in her hair chatted on her cell phone and made my car vibrate with her funky music. The sheer volume of cars on the road had swelled to epic proportions that February day as the snowbirds descended into Florida. I felt frazzled and irritated.

In fact, I realized that I felt wrought-up and stressed out entirely too often, and it wasn't only in traffic. Dishes piled on the counter instead of in the dishwasher? Hyperventilate. Unfolded laundry heaped over the recliner? Hyperventilate. Yet another doctor's appointment? Hyperventilate. Sassy kids? Don't even get me started.

Then one day God pointed out the common denominator in each one of these episodes: *me.* He clearly showed me an aptitude for wadding up my heart over issues grand and small. It's so easy for most of us to become stirred up when things don't go the way we'd like. The truth is God values "the unfading beauty of a gentle and quiet spirit, which is of great worth in God's sight" (1 Peter 3:4).

I've always secretly admired calm, sweet women who never seem to lose their cool. Somehow, they remain serene and composed regardless of the number of dishes crammed onto their kitchen counters.

First Peter 3:5 tells us that a gentle, peaceful spirit is how women of the day adorned themselves, "for this is the way the holy women of the past who put their hope in God used to adorn themselves." Take a moment to ask the Lord for your own customized beauty treatment. Write down specific areas in need of special attention, if you desire.

Inner beauty and charm are qualities we can't get from high-tech face creams and lotions. But when we choose to embrace meekness, we slather ourselves with a deep beauty treatment that never fails—one that keeps us charming even when the car behind us is threatening to drive right up our tailpipe. And *this* beauty treatment's effects are eternal.

Daily Prayer

Dear Lord,

I confess that my heart is "wrought up" on many occasions. Forgive me for allowing myself to become overly upset and stressed out. Please pour out Your Spirit on me and help me to come up higher in this area. Help me not to allow myself to be agitated and disturbed, and enable me to walk in meekness during even my tensest moments. When I sense myself moving towards anxiety and am tempted to hyperventilate, help me to take a deep breath, relax, and cry out to You for help. Alert me when I unknowingly begin to tense and veer toward distress so that I can choose to practice meekness through Your grace and power instead.

Lord, I know that You will not fail me or leave me without a way out. You are my example of meekness; help me to remain in Your shadow and cling to You in my weakness. Help me not to think of myself more highly than I ought to, and to consider others as greater than myself. Let me walk in peace and meekness instead of stress and agitation. Keep me calm, peaceful, tranquil, and serene, regardless of the situations I face.

Please grant me the unfading charm of a gentle and meek spirit, which is of great value in Your sight. I make the decision to cultivate this area of my life to bring You glory. Thank You for Your grace at work within me so that I can walk in meekness every day of my life. In Jesus's mighty name, amen.

God's Word for Me

I will do what is right and not give way to fear (1 Peter 3:6).

You give me power to hold myself calm in days of adversity (Psalm 94:13 AMP).

I have the effect of righteousness, which is peace [internal and external], quietness, and confident trust forever (Isaiah 32:17 AMP).

I have the unfading beauty of a gentle and quiet spirit, which is of great worth in God's sight (1 Peter 3:4).

I will pursue righteousness, godliness, faith, love,
endurance and gentleness (1 Timothy 6:11).

I will be completely humble and gentle; I will be
patient, bearing with others in love
(Ephesians 4:2).

In the multitude of my [anxious] thoughts,
Your comforts cheer and delight my soul
(Psalm 94:19 AMP).

My Dreams

As a young girl, my heart's desire was to live the normal life I saw my friends living. For me, that meant simple things like sheets on the mattresses, regular meals, clean clothes to wear every day, no more explosive anger, and toilet paper in the bathroom. Deep down, I strongly craved peace and stability.

My dream began to unfold years later, when I met Jesus. He loved me, thrilled me, and understood me like no one else. And slowly, hand-in-hand with Him, my dream to live a healthy, normal life started. But it wasn't easy.

A dream is easy—even thrilling—to envision. Dreaming the dream is the easy part! Yet often as we pursue our dream reality sets in, the thrill fades, and we find ourselves struggling, fighting, and feeling overwhelmed. Ecclesiastes 5:3 says, "For a dream comes with much business and painful effort" (AMP). In other words, no dream becomes a reality without a price.

As we strive toward our dreams, the enemy's strategy is to impede us so we won't fight for what is rightfully ours. Giants of Intimidation and Insecurity taunt us, just like Goliath taunted Israel.

First Samuel 17 shows the Israelites frozen with fear when confronted with Goliath, the Philistine giant from Gath. Standing nearly ten feet tall, Goliath wore custom armor that made him appear even more intimidating. No one dared stand up to him until a young shepherd boy heard his mocking words and decided enough was enough. David clearly heard the taunts of the enemy, but refused to believe them. David's relationship with the Lord was so real, so strong, that the enemy's boast meant nothing to him. A mere adolescent, he triumphed over the giant.

Are you a dream-chaser? When we run after our dreams, we will have to battle a few giants. Our success in slaying the giants in our lives is determined by…

1. **Our willingness to confront the enemy.** In verse 48, we see that David *ran quickly* to meet Goliath. No hesitation. No fear. Boldly. And with utter confidence.

2. **Our past successes with God.** In verses 34–37 David explains to Saul that he has already slain a lion and a bear. When we are intimidated by the enemy, we can remember past triumphs,

reminding ourselves of our God-given abilities and God's faithfulness.

3. **Knowing the Lord intimately.** David spent his days worshipping and conversing with God while he tended his father's flock. When we remain close to and intimate with the Lord, the enemy's taunts will never sway us.

4. **A confidence and understanding that the battle is the Lord's.** This doesn't excuse us from action and doing our part, but rather, reveals a deep knowing within us that God is our ultimate source and strength.

Daily Prayer

Dear Lord,

As I pursue Your will for my life and chase after my dreams, give me boldness to fearlessly confront and stand up to the enemy, when necessary, with boldness and confidence. Help me to remember my past successes through Your grace, and to know You more intimately. Help me to hear Your voice and understand Your character more clearly so that I will never be swayed by the enemy's taunts. There are many dreams and desires in my heart, Father. Please help me differentiate between the dreams You have given me and any dreams that are not authored by You. Help me to pursue the dreams for which You've equipped me and let go of the dreams that aren't part of Your plan.

I believe that the battle is Yours, God, but I want to do my part. Give me wisdom and understanding as I make every effort to become a dream-chaser committed to fulfilling my God-given destiny. Strengthen and equip me as I step forward while leaning entirely on You. In Your precious name, amen.

God's Word for Me

All my hard work brings a profit, but mere talk leads me only to poverty (Proverbs 14:23).

I will roll my works upon the Lord [and He will cause my thoughts to become agreeable to His will] so my plans will be established and succeed (Proverbs 16:3 AMP).

The end of a matter is better than its beginning,
and patience is better than pride (Ecclesiastes 7:8).

Whatever my hand finds to do, I will do it with all
my might (Ecclesiastes 9:10).

I will give careful thought to the paths for my feet
and be steadfast in all my ways (Proverbs 4:26).

In my heart I plan my course, but the Lord establishes my steps (Proverbs 16:9).

I will allow no [unnecessary] sleep to my eyes,
no slumber to my eyelids (Proverbs 6:4 AMP).

My Joy

When our glittering ten-foot Christmas tree crashed to the floor one December night, I hardly knew what to do first. Should I grab a towel for our now sodden carpet? Pick up the shattered ornaments before a sharp sliver punctured someone's foot? Or grab the vacuum cleaner and get busy on the 14,000 Frasier fir needles now flung across our living room?

Delegator extraordinaire, I ordered my daughter to grab towels and our son to get the vacuum cleaner. I gingerly lifted shards of silver and blue glass out of the carpet. My husband took on the Herculean effort of raising our hefty, frazzled tree.

When the mess was finally lifted up, sopped up, picked up, and vacuumed up, I stared at the array of ornaments still scattered across our sofa and felt my shoulders droop. Each one needed to be hung on our half-empty Christmas tree. Again. Exhausted from a hectic weekend, I groaned.

That was when our then 14-year-old daughter clapped her hands and jumped up and down. "We get to decorate our Christmas tree again!"

Sometimes joy is a matter of perspective. And that night, I discovered that joy is always a choice. Emily's beaming face challenged my Scrooge-like heart, and it made me think. What if the hard circumstances we're currently facing are really opportunities to find joy in an unlikely place? What if, instead of expecting everything to be perfect, we looked for the remarkable in life's imperfections?

Over two thousand years ago, wise men and kings traveled to find the Source of joy, disguised as an infant. Flies buzzed and fresh piles of manure steamed in the chilly night air. But when earthly kings knelt in the mud and straw, they received remarkable joy in the most unlikely place. And when I knelt on damp carpet to redecorate our Christmas tree that December night, so did I.

I think that's what Christmas—and our messy lives—are all about. We are on a journey, and the destination is the One through whom all joy ultimately flows.

Daily Prayer

Dear Lord,

Forgive me for allowing circumstances to gauge and affect my joy. Help me not to surrender my joy, but to maintain a godly perspective that allows me to persistently look for joy in the middle of life's messy moments. Enable me to remember, Jesus, that You said I could have life and life more abundant. I don't want to waste all that You accomplished for me, so help me to choose joy in unlikely places. Give me contagious joy that splashes onto those around me. And even when circumstances get ugly, help me to choose joy.

Give me Your fresh perspective so that I'm able to see joy in unlikely places. Please give me grace to walk in the fruit of the Spirit, which includes joy. As I spend time with You through prayer, worship, and reading Your word, continually fill me with Your joy. In the wonderful name of Jesus, amen.

God's Word for Me

For you make me glad by your deeds, Lord;
I sing for joy at what your hands have done
(Psalm 92:4).

You make known to me the path of life; you will
fill me with joy in your presence, with eternal
pleasures at your right hand (Psalm 16:11).

You have made known to me the paths of life; you
will fill me with joy in your presence (Acts 2:28).

I will be joyful in hope, patient in affliction,
faithful in prayer (Romans 12:12).

I will consider it pure joy whenever I face trials of
many kinds (James 1:2).

I will walk in the fruit of the Spirit, which is love,
joy, peace, forbearance, kindness, goodness,
faithfulness, gentleness and self-control
(Galatians 5:22-23).

Though I have not seen him, I love him; and even
though I do not see him now, I believe in him and
am filled with an inexpressible and glorious joy
(1 Peter 1:8).

My Humility

When a spatula-full of finely chopped veggies accidentally catapulted onto my left sandal, spilling over onto the floor, I groaned. Transferring minced onions, celery, and carrots out of the food processor and into a glass bowl turned out to be trickier than I thought.

Grabbing a paper towel, I knelt to scoop up the mess. That's when I noticed the sorry state of my kitchen floor.

Really sorry.

Only moments earlier it had looked fine. But with my face mere inches away from *scary* gunk, I gulped. What struck me is that my kneeling position left no escaping the truth. A single glance convinced me that my not-so-pristine kitchen floor could use a deep cleaning.

Likewise, humbly bowing and pausing our hearts before God allows Him to reveal any scary goop clinging there. Things might look fine on the surface, but our hearts are most likely in dire need of some heavy-duty scrubbing. "The heart is deceitful above all things, and it is exceedingly perverse and corrupt and severely, mortally sick!" (Jeremiah 17:9 AMP).

Kneeling is an outward sign of inner humility. It's a posture of reverent listening, as opposed to the distracted listening that frequently qualifies as today's normal. Kneeling gives us a completely different perspective—and sometimes that's exactly what we need. When we make time to pray, humbling our hearts and asking God to reveal the condition of our hearts, He will.

When we become aware of the state of our heart, it can leave us feeling surprised at all the icky stuff inside. I think one of the reasons God put this particular verse in the Bible is so we would understand our desperate need for a Savior and His cleansing blood. But God doesn't reveal our sin to condemn us; He reveals our sin so we can ask for forgiveness.

A truly humble heart is willing to look at and admit to the goop within. But then we gain great freedom and relief when we receive the forgiveness that only Jesus offers.

The next time I'm making pasta fagioli soup, I won't mind at all if I accidentally send sliced veggies flying over the edge of my kitchen's island. Because God knows I can always use a little more time on my knees.

Daily Prayer

Dear Lord,

Forgive me for the times I have acted proudly or in any way grieved Your Holy Spirit by words or actions that do not reflect the true humility of Jesus. Please grant me a humble, willing, obedient heart. Use the circumstances in my life to teach me humility, and help me to recognize and cooperate with You at all times, even when it's not pleasant.

Lord, I know You resist the proud. I don't want You to resist me, God, but I desire Your favor. As best as I know how, I willingly yield to the work You are doing in my heart and my life and humble myself before You. Please help me to embrace authentic humility. Help me to consider others as better than myself, and enable me to assume the guise of a servant, as Christ did. I desire for my life to genuinely reflect the humility of Christ. Enable me to walk in true humility by the power of Your Holy Spirit. In the precious name of Jesus, amen.

God's Word for Me

I will have the same attitude and purpose and [humble] mind which was in Christ Jesus. [He will be my example in humility] (Philippians 2:5 AMP).

I will be completely humble and gentle;
I will be patient, bearing with others in love
(Ephesians 4:2).

I will walk in humility, which is the fear of the LORD (Proverbs 22:4).

I will do nothing out of selfish ambition or vain conceit. Rather, in humility I will value others above myself. (Philippians 2:3).

I will clothe myself with humility toward others, because God opposes the proud but shows favor to the humble (1 Peter 5:5).

I will clothe myself with compassion, kindness, humility, gentleness and patience
(Colossians 3:12).

Pride will bring me low, but I will become lowly in spirit and gain honor (Proverbs 29:23).

My Love

I never truly realized what love was until I married—and then ran away. Instead of bliss, I felt acute misery and dark loneliness. My husband and I clashed from the very moment we said *I do.* Our honeymoon broke my heart; life afterwards was definitely *not* happily ever after. Through the years, I cried so many tears into God's bottle (see Psalm 56:8) I suspect He had to have it enlarged.

Deliriously unhappy, everything in me wanted to run hard and long. So I did.

Over and over I'd pile my suitcase into the car, desperate to get away from the tension, stress, and misery of my marriage. What I didn't yet realize was that although my husband's actions were wrong, my reactions were just as unjustified.

After I gave my life to Jesus, He began to influence me and change those unhealthy patterns like no one else could. Jesus's love soothed my aching heart, and I sensed His promise that somehow His love could make a difference in my marriage. Soon that whisper of a promise inched closer until I could smell it, like you can smell the rain before a drop has yet fallen. But it didn't turn out to be the magic wand I thought it would be. Instead, the Lord wanted me to live out and truly learn the various facets of His love.

The first love facet turned out to be patience, and it ripened in me through years of waiting, longing, and believing that God could transform a broken, lifeless marriage. Patience told me not to give up, not to leave. *Love is patient.*

Then the Lord taught me to walk in the facet of love which willingly lets go of an offense instead of keeping score. Letting go is never easy, but *Love keeps no record of wrong.*

He gently encouraged me to use kind words when my flesh wanted to lash out with a stinging retort. *Love is kind.*

He enabled me to admit a wrongdoing and sincerely apologize. *Love is not proud.*

He caused me to reflect His thoughtful demeanor and consider my husband's feelings before my own. *Love is not rude.*

God also taught me that true love isn't like a newborn, all wrapped up in itself and constantly making loud demands. *Love is not self-seeking.*

But mostly, God taught me that because of His

love, all things are possible. Things like celebrating a twenty-fifth wedding anniversary against all odds. *Love never fails.* I never truly realized what love was until I married—and stayed married—by the power of God's amazing love.

Daily Prayer

Father,

I confess that my perception of love is often vastly different from its reality, and I ask You to change that. Help me to let go of inaccurate, preconceived ideas about love and embrace authentic love, the kind of love that lays down its life by Your grace. Help me to experience Your love, which far surpasses mere knowledge. Enable me to comprehend the breadth and length and height and depth of Your amazing love.

Transform me through Your love, and make me a glowing example of Your lovingkindness. Give me Your love for not only my husband and family members, but for all people. Enable me to walk in love in difficult situations, always choosing loving responses that honor You and reveal Your love at work in me. I pray that through Your love, I will always be willing to believe the best of every person, avoid jealous or haughty behavior, and bear up under everything that comes. Help me to demonstrate the facets of Your love at work in my life by exhibiting patience, kindness, and unfading hope. Thank You for Your unfailing love at work in me. In the precious name of Jesus, amen.

God's Word for Me

God's love within me helps me to always protect, always trust, always hope, always persevere (1 Corinthians 13:7).

I am coming to know this love that surpasses knowledge, and I am filled to the measure of all the fullness of God (Ephesians 3:19).

I will be glad and rejoice in your unfailing love, for you have seen my troubles, and you care about the anguish of my soul (Psalm 31:7 NLT).

I will sing of your strength, in the morning I will sing of your love; for you are my fortress, my refuge in times of trouble (Psalm 59:16).

I will love the Lord my God with all my heart and with all my soul and with all my strength and with all my mind. And I will love my neighbor as myself (Luke 10:27).

I will love others as Christ has loved me (John 13:34).

For I am convinced that nothing will be able to separate me from the love of God which is in Christ Jesus my Lord (Romans 8:38-39).

My Physical Health

A *suspicious mass?* I stared at my doctor's face, willing my mind to understand his shocking words. Just moments earlier I had undergone a diagnostic ultrasound due to insanely stubborn female problems. My husband and I had watched as the technician zeroed in on a particular area in my abdomen that pulsated with colors. We had no clue what she saw, but our concern mounted.

Immediately ushered into my doctor's office to go over the results, Keith and I stared out the eighth-floor window with a sweeping view of Sarasota Bay. Boats glided over sun-speckled water, but my anxiety intruded on the lovely scene. Soon my doctor walked in and seated himself behind his massive wooden desk.

As he began talking, my heart sank. "It appears as though your left ovary has migrated down…" Migrated? One of my body parts had *migrated*? I took a deep breath and tried to concentrate. "…and is surrounded by copious vascular tissue which has formed into what we consider to be a suspicious mass."

My husband and I looked at each other, dumbfounded. Of all the things I probably never expected to hear in my lifetime, a migrating suspicious mass probably topped the list. Leaning forward, I peered at the lavishly colored photo of my insides. Looking up into my doctor's eyes, I asked, "What do you recommend, and what are my options?" My belly quivered. Not *another* surgery. *Oh God, please.*

Unfortunately, my doctor *did* need to perform surgery to discover what on earth was going on inside me. He felt optimistic due to my age and general good health, but I was overwhelmed at the thought of a fourth surgery for this ongoing issue.

Though things don't always turn out for us healthwise as we wish they would, we have the power of prayer to uphold us. I always ask God to intervene in every medical situation, from a slight cold to more serious issues, such as my migrating ovary. God has the ability and power to physically heal us, and though He doesn't always say yes, I don't think that should prevent us from asking.

While we cannot always control what disease or accidents befall us, we can make wise choices that directly impact our physical health. Though we all have different bodies and each of us faces different issues physically, a healthy diet, good sleep habits, regular exercise, and effectively managing stress can improve our overall quality of life. As we make our best efforts in the areas over which we do have control and diligently pray and trust God in areas we don't, our physical health will be the best that it can be this side of heaven.

Daily Prayer

Dear Lord,

You've given me this sometimes fragile tent to wear here on earth, and I lift it up to You, the Great Physician. Please strengthen my body and grant me divine health. Help me to use wisdom regarding my body and my health. Enable me to make wise choices that do not bring harm, but that bring life and promote vivacious well-being.

You know the issues in my body, Lord. I stand in agreement with You for complete healing. I plead the blood of Jesus over every bone, joint, muscle, tendon, ligament, organ, hormone, system, and cell in my body. I believe that by the stripes of Jesus I am healed and made whole. Regardless of the afflictions that I deal with in my body, Lord, I commit to serving You to the best of my ability, not using physical issues as an excuse, but allowing them to humble me and propel me deeper into Your presence. In the name of Jesus I thank You for healing and restoring every area of my body through Your mercy, lovingkindness, and amazing power. Amen.

God's Word for Me

My faith has healed me. I will go in peace and be freed from my suffering (Mark 5:34).

I believe, God, that you are restoring me to health and healing my wounds (Jeremiah 30:17).

I will focus on your gracious words, which are a honeycomb, sweet to my soul and healing to my bones (Proverbs 16:24).

He was pierced for my transgressions, he was crushed for my iniquities; the punishment that brought me peace was on him, and by his wounds I am healed (Isaiah 53:5).

He sent out his word and healed me
(Psalm 107:20).

He forgives all my sins and heals all my diseases
(Psalm 103:3).

Heal me, Lord, and I will be healed; save me and
I will be saved, for you are the one I praise
(Jeremiah 17:14).

My Wisdom

I sat on the edge of my bed, arms crossed, while my irritated mind played tug-of-war. I wanted to march out into the family room and give my husband *what for*. His angry words catapulted me over the edge, and how could he *know* how much he upset me unless I *told* him? It was past 11 p.m., I was tired beyond reason, and the teeny warning light flickering inside my heart was begging me not to do it, but these did nothing to dissuade me.

Walking to the bedroom door, I took a deep breath, mentally preparing to unleash on the man who dared to treat me wrong. Heaven help us both.

An hour later, I clung to the edge of the mattress, rigid and miserable. My husband hadn't responded to my tirade about *his* tirade with any measure of understanding. Our heated words had flared into a towering inferno whose sparks rekindled issues and more issues. Before I knew it flames of anger had engulfed us both, and both our hearts were singed to a crisp.

If only I had used wisdom.

Unfortunately, it took me a long time to figure out that if I wanted to approach my husband about a matter, I needed to use wisdom. In my heart, I desperately desired conflict resolution. However, wisdom meant not only waiting until *I* had cooled down, but *not* waiting until moments before bed to bring up a potentially explosive issue. Wisdom tells us when (and what) to speak; it also leads us to be quiet at the appropriate time. Wisdom equips us for the bumps, surprises, and sticky issues that take us by surprise. Wisdom prevents us from unintentionally lighting bonfires in our family room.

Wisdom also protects us, guides us, and enables us to respond instead of react to volatile situations. First Samuel 17:17-30 is an outstanding example of wisdom at work. King David, just a teenager, visited his brothers out on the battlefield at his father's request. His dad simply wanted word about how his brothers fared, so he loaded David with bread and cheese and sent him to get the scoop. But… "When Eliab, David's oldest brother, heard him speaking with the men, he burned with anger at him and asked, 'Why did you come down here? And with whom did you leave those few sheep in the wilderness? I know how conceited you are and how wicked your heart is; you came down only to watch the battle.'"

Instead of launching into defense mode and whacking his brother upside the head with an angry response, Scripture shows a wise response. "Now what have I done? Can't I even speak?" Wisdom reminds us that a soft answer prevents words from escalating and leads us on the right path. Best of all, when we partner with wisdom we partner with Jesus Himself, who *is* Wisdom.

Daily Prayer

Father,

Your word says that if I lack wisdom, all I need to do is ask You, and You will give it to me. God, I need wisdom. Please grant me wisdom for the situations I'm facing today. Give me insight and understanding for the relationship issues I'm dealing with, and help me to continually use wisdom as situations and concerns arise. I pray that wisdom will be my default mode, and that I will avoid foolish arguments and controversies.

Help me to respond and not react. Give me the wisdom to turn away from inflammatory remarks, avoid taking offense, and to know what to do and how to respond in every situation. Help me resist being drawn into situations through foolish choices. Give me wisdom as I deal with my spouse, my children, and other family members. I pray that Your wisdom will direct and guide me as I relate to coworkers, neighbors, and friends, and even while I drive in crazy traffic. Fill me with Your wisdom so that my thoughts, words, and actions reflect and please You. In Jesus's mighty name, amen.

God's Word for Me

I will commit to the Lord whatever I do, and he will establish my plans (Proverbs 16:3).

I will not be vague, thoughtless, or foolish, but I will understand and firmly grasp the will of the Lord (Ephesians 5:17 AMP).

My gentle answer turns away wrath, but my harsh word stirs up anger (Proverbs 15:1).

My mouth will speak words of wisdom; the meditation of my heart will give understanding (Psalm 49:3).

When I lack wisdom, I will ask God,
who gives generously (James 1:5).

God will instruct me in the way of wisdom and
lead me along straight paths (Proverbs 4:11 AMP).

I will not let wisdom and understanding out of
my sight; I will preserve sound judgment and
discretion (Proverbs 3:21).

My Emotions

One gorgeous summer evening, I interrupted my daughter's outdoor playtime for a mere bath. Her indignant body language—crossed arms and an extruded lower lip—foretold an unpleasant bathing experience in my immediate future. I settled her three-year-old body into the tub anyway and asked her to hand me the bar of soap floating behind her.

Minutes passed in tumultuous silence as my little girl attempted to grip the bobbing soap while fending off tears. Finally, she looked up at me and with a whimper said, "I'm trying not to cry, Mommy, but my *self* won't let me!"

I know the feeling. Emotions have a way of overwhelming me sometimes too. Then, they like to hang on much longer than they are welcome. Of course, there is a time for everything, including tears. But I don't want my emotions controlling me any more than I wanted my three-year-old calling the shots.

The truth is God gave us emotions. They flavor our lives like savory spices flavor a hearty stew. Yet in the span of 24 hours a woman's emotions can soar from delight and giddy laughter down to heartfelt tears and indignation—and back again. If you factor in achingly sweet background music, certain days of the month, and whether or not there is chocolate in the house, well, watch out.

If we're not careful, raw emotions can control us and potentially lead us down a destructive path. God's word is not only the plumb line for our responses, but a safety restraint that will prevent us from flying through our heart's dashboard windshield when we're emotional wrecks.

King David may have been a man after God's own heart, but he is also someone I can completely relate to. This warrior-psalmist was a Renaissance man of emotions, but he refused to allow his feelings to be in charge. He actually talked to himself when his emotions started to take over, and for some reason, I like that. David was not afraid to confront his emotions—and then speak truth to himself, loud and clear.

Let's face it: There will be days when our emotions need a good talking-to. There are moments when we need to tell ourselves *Girl, get a grip! It's going to be okay! Keep your focus on God and praise Him anyway!* With God's help, we really *can* control our raw emotions instead of allowing them to control us.

Daily Prayer

Dear Lord,

Thank You for the gift of my emotions. Through them, I experience joy, delight, satisfaction, and peace—and many other feelings. I appreciate the wonder of the full spectrum of emotions You have enabled me to experience.

But I confess there are times when I allow my emotions to get the best of me, and instead of controlling them, my emotions seem to control me. Please help me not to allow myself to be led entirely by my emotions, but instead be led by Your Holy Spirit and wisdom. Though I'm a woman subject to hormones and sensitivity, enable me to walk in the Spirit and not in the flesh. Help me not to allow myself to become agitated and disturbed, but to walk in the power of Your peace, even in the middle of anxiety-producing events.

When my emotions threaten to overwhelm me, help me to bring them to You, as King David did, and process them with You. Help me to be authentic with You and entrust my emotions to You, because You understand my thoughts and emotions, Lord. Give me godly perspective and the ability to hold myself calm in days of adversity, Father. And help me to glorify You even when my emotions get messy. In Jesus's mighty name, amen.

God's Word for Me

You, LORD, are a shield around me, my glory, the One who lifts my head high (Psalm 3:3).

You give me the power to keep myself calm in the days of adversity (Psalm 94:13 AMP).

Do not withhold your mercy from me, LORD; may your love and faithfulness always protect me (Psalm 40:11).

Have mercy on me, LORD; heal me, for I have sinned against you (Psalm 41:4).

My soul is in deep anguish. How long, LORD, how long? (Psalm 6:3).

I am poor and needy; may the Lord think of me. You are my help and my deliverer; you are my God, do not delay (Psalm 40:17).

All my longings lie open before you, Lord; my sighing is not hidden from you (Psalm 38:9).

My Past

While waiting at the airport on a long layover, I enjoyed watching all the unique, cool-looking luggage rolling past me. From a fun giraffe motif to serious plaid, from basic black to bags that glittered, the suitcases scooted past, many with high-lift handles that accommodated smaller suitcases stacked on top. My favorite by far featured spinner wheels that moved in every direction with ease.

With the high cost of checking luggage these days, more and more people are carrying their bags with them on the plane. But the problem with taking my luggage on board instead of checking it at the front of the airport is it slows me down. I've envied many a traveler gliding effortlessly sans suitcase through airport security. Regardless of the fancy wheels, zippy handles, and handy compartments, suitcases still have to be lugged from one destination to the next. And have you ever attempted to use the public ladies' room while lugging your suitcase? Definitely not convenient.

Similarly, baggage from our past is a hindrance on the tarmac of our lives. And many times, we don't even realize we're still toting heavy, bulging burdens. We've simply become accustomed to their girth and weight. But that has never been God's plan for us. In fact, I believe the Lord is asking us to check our earthly luggage—with Him. Luke 10:4 says, "Do not take a purse or bag or sandals..." Sounds like *no suitcases* to me! I believe one of the reasons the disciples were told by Jesus not to carry their belongings is He wanted them to travel light. And *that* is our example.

If the road is narrow, why do we always overpack for the trip? Whether it's a twenty-year-old hurt or a grudge from last week, past issues are still baggage, and they can potentially hinder our progress as we attempt to move forward. Every time we use our past to excuse our behavior, hold on to an offense, or refuse to forgive, we're clutching the very things that threaten to hold us back. Who wants to struggle through life with overstuffed suitcases banging into their ankles? It's exhausting!

In contrast, Jesus tells us in Matthew 11:30, "My yoke is easy and my burden is light." God created us to travel light.

The Lord wants nothing to impede our spiritual progress or distract our focus. He wants us to move ahead unencumbered by the pain of our past. As we release our past into His hands, He will relieve us, help us, and work out our past for our good and for His glory.

Daily Prayer

Father,

You alone know the issues and hurts of my heart. It is not my desire to hold on to painful things from my past, intentional or not. So today I'm asking You to move in my heart. Search my heart and know me, and reveal to me any vestiges of the past that have left a residue inside me. Sweep through me with Your mighty love and bring healing, wholeness, and restoration.

Show me areas of hurt that I need to surrender to You. Enable me to release the things to which I cling, things I may not even be aware of. Help me to cooperate with the workings of Your Holy Spirit so that I am unencumbered and can travel light, moving forward with ease and in Your grace. Remove and heal the remnants of every painful memory. Jesus, Your yoke is easy and Your burden is light, and those are the only bags with which I wish to travel. As I willingly let go of every piece of baggage You reveal to me, flood me with Your peace, Your joy, and Your unfailing love, and enable me to travel light, moving forward in Your amazing grace. In Your wonderful name, amen.

God's Word for Me

I will throw off everything that hinders and the sin that so easily entangles. And I will run with perseverance the race marked out for me (Hebrews 12:1).

I am in Christ, and have become a new person. My old life is gone and my new life has begun! (2 Corinthians 5:17 NLT).

I will fix my eyes on Jesus (Hebrews 12:2).

I will put off my old self, which is corrupted by its deceitful desires (Ephesians 4:22).

There is no condemnation because I am in Christ Jesus (Romans 8:1).

I will cast all my anxiety on You because You care for me (1 Peter 5:7).

When I walk, my steps will not be hampered; when I run, I will not stumble (Proverbs 4:12).

My Peace

Emotions swirled and tears stung my eyes the day my oldest son announced that he had enlisted with the U.S. Army. Just two months after the 9/11 terrorist attacks, I couldn't help but feel proud of him. Yet at the same time I wanted to shake him. Especially when he told me he had signed up for the infantry. (That's code for front-line soldiers with guns.) Why couldn't he just sell life insurance instead?

Several months later my worst fears materialized as the president declared war on Iraq. Soon, our 20-year-old son was in the middle of the Iraqi desert with the 3rd Infantry Division. At the time, it was believed that Iraq's dictator, Saddam Hussein, possessed an arsenal of nuclear weapons. Fear gripped me as I realized that if the enemy dropped a nuclear bomb anywhere in the vicinity, the entire 3rd I.D. would be wiped out, and I would never see my boy again.

I had always considered myself a praying woman who trusted God. Yet as my son prepared for battle, I became engulfed in a gut-wrenching assault on the trust I claimed to possess. In the middle of a mother's nightmare, I struggled to walk in peace.

You may not have a son or daughter serving in the military, but you're probably familiar with the battle for peace nonetheless. Whether you are facing serious marital issues, health setbacks, financial troubles, or other difficulties, there are seasons for everything. These are stressful, not-so-pleasant times we'd probably rather not endure. But the truth is, those times come to all of us. And sometimes the battle is so intense we become overwhelmed. Instead of walking in peace, we give in and freak out.

I believe that the key to peace during times of crisis, conflict, and our overwhelming situations can be found in 2 Chronicles 20:3-22. King Jehoshaphat discovered that a massive army was headed his way. Besieged in more ways than one, he cried out to God, and then assumed his position—of worship. And God moved. Verse 22 says, "As they began to sing and praise, the LORD set ambushes against the men of Ammon and Moab and Mount Seir who were invading Judah, and they were defeated."

On the tenth day of Operation Iraqi Freedom, sleep-deprived and weak from a complete loss of appetite, I knew something had to give. Desperate for

God's peace, I turned on a worship CD, lifted my arms, and sang praise. And God moved. His awesome presence flooded my soul. Laughter bubbled out of me and peace flooded me. From that point on, I never worried about my son—not even once! Oh, I prayed for him. You'd better believe I regularly thought of Jason and prayed for him—sometimes hourly. But miraculously, I truly never felt worried about him during the remainder of his deployment.

Worshipping in a time of crisis flies in the face of all we're feeling. Our emotions tempt us to have a meltdown. Yet when we choose to shift our focus from the overwhelming situation to the Lord, when we worship *in spite* of how we're feeling, we move the heart of God. He will intervene. And though the circumstance may not change (my son was still in Iraq, after all), *we* will change. We will have peace in the middle of our battles. And no matter how hard he tries, the enemy will not be able to rattle us. I won the battle for peace through worship, and I'm confident that you can too.

Daily Prayer

Oh God,

I desire to walk in peace in every situation. I don't want to be moved by my circumstances, shaken and upset by the things going on around me. Help me not to allow myself to be agitated and disturbed, but to choose Your presence and the precious peace Jesus bequeathed to me in the middle of every circumstance.

Help me to remember that Your peace is always available to me. Give me grace to realize in the middle of the battle that all I need to do is shift my focus and worship You, the lover of my soul. Help me to follow after and be led by peace at all times—when I'm making decisions, in conversations, when the unexpected happens. Flood my heart and emotions with Your overwhelming peace during every circumstance. And help me to be a light shining for You, Lord. When I walk in peace during hard situations, my family, friends and neighbors have the opportunity to witness the reality of the Prince of Peace at work. May others be drawn to You because Your peace within me is so clearly evident in my life. In the wonderful name of Jesus, amen.

God's Word for Me

You have bequeathed Your peace to me,
Jesus. I will not let my heart be troubled or let it
be afraid (John 14:27 AMP).

You have rescued me unharmed from the battle
waged against me (Psalm 55:18).

You will keep me in perfect peace because
I trust in you (Isaiah 26:3).

In peace I will lie down and sleep, for you alone,
LORD, make me dwell in safety (Psalm 4:8).

My ways are pleasant ways, and all my paths
are peace (Proverbs 3:17).

I will let the peace of Christ rule in my heart,
since as a member of one body I was called to
peace (Colossians 3:15).

As far as it depends on me, I will live at peace with
everyone (Romans 12:18).

My Value

I couldn't understand it. Over many weeks, the Lord had made it unmistakably clear that I was to lovingly confront a family member about a particular issue. With no aspiration to be a boat-rocker, I prayed and waited, receiving multiple confirmations that this was what I needed to do. Even then, I talked it through with my husband and sought a way out. *Couldn't we just forget the whole thing, Lord?* But in the end, God made His will for me to speak up in this particular situation so obvious I had no choice.

Unfortunately, things did not go well. I had stepped so far outside my comfort zone I felt like I was in a new zip code. I carefully bookended my words with kindness, but sadly, the response was flat-out denial. My heart sank. I had done my part, but my words were met with a traffic cop's raised hand. At that point, the issue simply could not be resolved.

Of course I felt upset, yet surprisingly, what bothered me most was not the lack of family harmony or resolution. What concerned me was the bewildering spectrum of wild emotions the whole scenario triggered deep inside me. I began to second-guess myself; I felt like an insecure little girl, frightened and deeply disturbed. Yet I had no idea why.

Rattled, I spent many days in prayer, asking God to reveal to me the root cause of my perplexing, visceral response. His answer couldn't have surprised me more.

God clearly allowed me to perceive that as a child I felt unheard, not valued. This sparked a revelation: The little girl in me still longed to feel valued, to know that her words mattered—that *she* mattered. And I believe every one of us wants that same assurance.

The truth is, we matter deeply to God. On a walk one evening as I processed these events, the Lord flooded my heart with the intimate revelation that He cherishes me, my words, and my thoughts. *I value you, Julie,* He whispered to me over and over. *I value you.* Tears gently rolled down my face as I drank in the words I so desperately needed to hear.

God values us, His children, above all else. In fact, He is always listening to us, we are the apple of His eye, He loves us with an everlasting love, and He sings over us with love.

What a priceless, beautiful gift! To know, *truly know* within the deepest part of our hearts that we are valued by the Creator of the Universe. He esteems us. He values us. And that's more than enough.

Daily Prayer

Dear Lord,

Thank You, Father, for placing such a high value on me that You sent Your precious Son, Jesus, to die for me. You paid a great price for me because You greatly prize me.

Please go to the deep places in me that have been hurt as a result of not feeling valued and cherished by others and bring healing. But even more, fill me with the acute awareness that I am Your beloved, and that You regard me as precious. Help me to understand and grasp that You are crazy in love with me! Flood my heart with the revelation of Your mighty, unfailing love. Enable me to perceive the depth to which You value me as Your daughter, and help me to walk securely in that knowledge all the days of my life. Oh Lord, thank You for esteeming me. You have tattooed my picture on the palm of Your hand and You cherish me, love me, and enjoy me. I intend to bask in Your loving presence as a child basks in her parents' doting smiles. In Jesus's precious name, amen.

God's Word for Me

I will cast all my anxiety on him
because he cares for me (1 Peter 5:7).

I am well-known and recognized [by God]
(2 Corinthians 6:9 AMP).

You thrill me, LORD, with all you have done for me! I sing for joy because of what you have done (Psalm 92:4 NLT).

I am precious and honored in God's sight,
and He loves me (Isaiah 43:4).

God has engraved me on the palms of his hands (Isaiah 49:16).

You have searched me, LORD, and you know me (Psalm 139:1).

I will weep no more. How gracious he will be when I cry for help! As soon as he hears, he will answer me (Isaiah 30:19).

God's Timing in My Life

Joshua tended our lush butterfly garden with surprising exuberance. What began as a temporary hobby blossomed into a passion for our then eight-year-old son. Vivid lantana, Mexican petunias, and a plethora of other unique, vibrant flowers drew an abundance of butterflies into our backyard. Stunning swallowtails, wispy white admirals, buckeyes, and monarchs fluttered among our flowers and into our daily conversations.

So when our family visited a traveling butterfly exhibit one Saturday afternoon, we splurged on the purchase of a rare caterpillar not typically found in our area. We placed handfuls of leafy branches, the caterpillar's food supply, inside a well-watered vase right next to his makeshift home on our fireplace mantel. Over the next two weeks we watched the little guy grow plumper by the day as he stripped every branch. Soon the caterpillar crawled to the top of a stem and a chrysalis formed. In just a few weeks, a rare butterfly would emerge. We could hardly wait to meet him and then release him into our garden.

One week passed, then two. Every morning we checked the chrysalis, to no avail. The third week came and went with no movement or signs of life, and soon we approached the one-month mark. Experience told us to be patient, yet we all began to wonder if something had gone wrong.

"I think the butterfly is dead," Joshua groaned after two long months had passed. I agreed. The chrysalis had never opened to reveal the new life within. Instead, a disgusting mold covered the cocoon.

"I don't understand what went wrong," I sighed, hugging my son close. The small plastic habitat now held nothing but brown water, dried leaves, and a rotting cocoon. Our expensive endeavor had come to nothing.

I intended to toss the entire mess, yet our mantel stood in a distant corner of the house. There the tiny habitat and its repulsive contents remained; a sad, forgotten eyesore shoved off to the side of our crazy lives.

Three months later I hurried past our fireplace on a cleaning mission when an unexpected movement caught my eye. Approaching the forlorn cup, I inhaled sharply. Where once a moldy chrysalis had hung, a spectacular new butterfly now shimmered. Stunned, I called Joshua, who jumped up and down in baffled joy.

We laughed in wonder, amazed at this unlikely turn of events. We had resigned ourselves to disappointment, yet God clearly was not finished working.

Often God's timing can appear much like the moldy chrysalis: too late. But the truth is, it's never too late for the Lord to intervene. Though it will cost us, in the end it will be worth the wait. While we may never entirely understand God's timing this side of heaven, we can trust that God alone can accomplish the seemingly impossible.

Though it might seem that God has allowed something in our life to expire, it may yet burst forth. The bottom line is, even when we struggle with God's timing, He is faithful. He will accomplish His plan in our lives, regardless of how things appear to us. Because deep within, in the hidden, secret places, God is always at work.

Daily Prayer

Heavenly Father,

I confess that I sometimes struggle with Your timing. I don't understand and struggle to believe that You are truly at work in spite of how things may appear. I long to relax and be at peace with Your timing instead of trying to control things or push things forward outside of Your perfect timing. I confess that I frequently want things now. But God, I don't want to be impatient or force events outside of Your timing. Please help me to grow in confident trust in You instead of freaking out and reacting wrong when things don't go according to my plans.

Help me to surrender my desire for control and truly believe that Your timing is far better than anything I can manipulate or conjure. Thank You, Lord, for Your faithfulness. Thank You for working in ways I cannot fully understand or appreciate. Right now I choose to trust Your timing in every situation I'm currently facing. I trust that You are moving and accomplishing Your plans and purpose in my life. In the precious name of Jesus, amen.

God's Word for Me

God will make this happen, for he who calls me is faithful (1 Thessalonians 5:24 NLT).

May your unfailing love with me, Lord, even as I
put my hope in you (Psalm 33:22).

Let Your mercy and loving-kindness, O Lord,
be upon us, in proportion to our waiting and
hoping for You (Ecclesiastes 3:1 AMP).

God changes my times and seasons (Daniel 2:21).

In all your ways know, recognize, and acknowledge Him, and He will direct and make straight
and plain your paths (Proverbs 3:6 AMP).

I will not become weary in doing good,
for at the proper time I will reap a harvest if I do
not give up (Galatians 6:9).

In you, LORD, I have taken refuge; let me never
be put to shame; deliver me in your righteousness
(Psalm 31:1).

My Mouth

It was just a simple phone call. Surely I could plead my case with a reasonable representative and the issue would be quickly and completely resolved. Just two weeks after a serious shoulder surgery, my insurance company was questioning my need for physical therapy. My physical therapist was incredulous. "How do they expect you to heal properly without ongoing therapy?" She shook her head.

I was deeply concerned that my left shoulder would never regain its full range of motion. The therapy itself was nothing short of torture, but if that's what it took, I'd keep eating ibuprofen and pushing myself to the limit. After suffering with a painfully injured shoulder for years, I was determined to do my part in the recuperation process—assuming I could get this insurance miscommunication cleared up.

However, the insurance rep refused to back down. When she mistakenly thought I had undergone a minor procedure and then refused to authorize further physical therapy appointments, I lost it. Apparently two weeks of unrelenting post-surgical pain, agonizing therapy, and the head-banging frustration of a misinformed insurance rep pushed me beyond my limit. And let's just say my response was not lovely.

Matthew 15:18 says, "the things that come out of a person's mouth come from the heart." Clearly some ugly stuff lurked in the depths of mine. Sometimes it takes a lot of pressure for our hearts to regurgitate their foul contents through our mouths. And though what comes spewing out of our mouths may surprise us, it does not surprise God—He can read our hearts, after all (see John 2:25).

It is a wise, mature woman who controls her tongue. Though James 3:8 says that no man can tame his tongue—and that certainly proved true for me that day with the insurance phone call—that doesn't mean we shouldn't make every effort to restrain our mouths. The only way this is possible is through the power of the Holy Spirit. If we can do all things through Christ, who strengthens us (see Philippians 4:13), then equipped by His grace, we *can* control our mouths.

As we determine to practice governing our mouths, I believe God will help us to honor Him and those around us when we speak. Then, instead of cleaning up collateral damage left in its wake, our mouths will leave a trail of kindness and encouragement.

Daily Prayer

Dear Lord,

Forgive me for allowing any harsh, hurtful, or unedifying words to come out of my mouth; I don't want to grieve You or hurt others. I truly desire to control my mouth and ask for Your grace to improve in this area. Please help me to walk in greater self-control, thinking and pausing before I say words I will regret. Help me to bless and not curse with my mouth. If out of the heart the mouth speaks, then Lord, I ask You to clean and purify my heart so that hurtful, ugly words will not erupt out of my mouth. Do a deep work, Lord, so that nothing ugly is left in my heart. May my words be edifying and encouraging to all those who hear them.

And Lord, help me not to speak against myself, particularly when I feel frustrated and doubt my ability to do what You are asking of me. Help me never to call myself names or use my mouth in any way to agree with the enemy. Thank You for enabling me to use my mouth for good—to speak positive, encouraging words to myself and to those around me. I determine right now to speak kindly to myself and to others. In Jesus's name, amen.

God's Word for Me

I will guard my mouth and my tongue and keep myself from calamity (Proverbs 21:23).

I will watch my ways and keep my tongue from sin; I will put a muzzle on my mouth (Psalm 39:1).

I have hidden your word in my heart that I might not sin against you (Psalm 119:11).

I speak with wisdom, and faithful instruction is on my tongue (Proverbs 31:26).

My lips will not say anything wicked, and my tongue will not utter lies (Job 27:4).

I will keep my tongue from evil and my lips from telling lies (Psalm 34:13).

My tongue will proclaim your righteousness, your praises all day long (Psalm 35:28).

My Thoughts

Have you ever thought about your thoughts? I mean, truly dissected your thoughts and wondered where they came from, as well as whether or not you should allow them to continue?

Sometimes our thoughts are like bad habits. We just absently think them, oblivious to any potential damage or negative effects they create.

Sometimes our thoughts are like open season for the enemy. He sees an opportunity to plant a wrong thought and steps across the line, knowing that we will allow him to trespass.

And sometimes our thoughts are the results of what the Bible calls gratifying the cravings and desires of the flesh (see Galatians 5:16). Whichever category our thoughts most often fall into, we can harness them and cause them to line up with God's word.

One of my biggest thought challenges involves my physical appearance. Healthy and thin my entire life, I was diagnosed with hypothyroidism six years ago after a multitude of symptoms hit me, including cramping muscles, extreme fatigue and (horrors)…weight gain, even though I hadn't made any changes in my diet.

Thankfully my doctor recognized my symptoms, tested me, and got me started on medication. The good news is, most days I feel great. The bad news is, my medication occasionally requires an adjustment, an unpleasant trial-and-error time involving blood work and increasing my dosage until I feel normal. But for me the worst part is how all this has affected my appearance. I'm not the thin woman I used to be. I struggle to feel beautiful carrying extra weight that simply refuses to budge, no matter how many miles I walk.

There are days when this invisible tug-of-war wears me down. But the good news is we always have a choice where our thoughts are concerned. Like a police officer standing in the middle of a busy four-corner intersection when the traffic lights have failed, we have authority to direct our thoughts in one direction or another. And like the motorists the officer is directing, our thoughts will comply and line up—if we direct them.

Our thoughts hold the potential to steer us in many directions. Let's pray this week that we will regularly patrol and direct our thoughts in a healthy, edifying, God-pleasing direction.

Daily Prayer

Dear Lord,

Help me to become discerning and aware of my thoughts, and not allow myself to fall into the bad habit of entertaining potentially damaging or negative thoughts. When I begin to think wrong thoughts, please alert me so that I can recognize them and choose to change my thoughts immediately. Right now I erect a *No Trespassing* sign over my thoughts to prevent Satan from taking advantage of any opportunity that might present itself in my thoughts. I will keep myself alert and aware by the power of Your Holy Spirit and resist every thought that does not line up with Your word.

Please enable me to walk in the Spirit and not gratify the cravings and desires of my flesh through my thoughts. When I veer off course, help me to get back on track. By Your grace, I will walk in the Spirit. Thank You for helping me to patrol and direct my thoughts in a healthy, edifying direction that pleases You, Lord. In Jesus's name, amen.

God's Word for Me

When anxiety is great within me, your consolation brings me joy (Psalm 94:19).

I will walk by the Spirit and not gratify the desires of the flesh (Galatians 5:16).

Search me, God, and know my heart; test me and know my anxious thoughts (Psalm 139:23).

I will walk blamelessly, do what is righteous, and speak the truth from my heart (Psalm 15:2).

If anything is excellent or praiseworthy—
I will think about such things (Philippians 4:8).

Direct and establish my heart toward You, Lord (1 Chronicles 29:18).

I will commit to the LORD whatever I do, and he will establish my plans (Proverbs 16:3).

My Identity

I awoke at 3:30 a.m., untangled my feet from the sheets as I sat up, and attempted to untangle the meaning of a dream—the same dream I'd experienced for years. The details varied, but the story was always the same: I set my purse down somewhere, thinking it was safe, and it got ransacked. My wallet was either stolen or everything in my wallet completely removed—my credit cards, driver's license, debit card. All gone.

My heart in turmoil, I prayed, asking God to show me the meaning of this recurring dream. Finally, the interpretation descended into my heart, and I was stunned. God helped me to understand that my purse and wallet held my personal information, my identity, and that my identity as His daughter—my identity in Christ, was being stolen. Worse yet, I was allowing the theft by leaving my purse (identity) in an unsafe place.

I began to understand that for far too long I had been listening to and believing the lies of the enemy without realizing it…the spiritual equivalent of leaving my purse wide open and unattended in a public place. I realized that every time I allowed the enemy to make me feel unworthy, unloved, ashamed, or not as good as someone else, it was the spiritual equivalent of opening my wallet in front of a thief, setting it down, and walking away.

Of course none of us would ever intentionally just leave our purses unguarded or hand our wallets to a potential thief. But every one of us can benefit from becoming spiritually alert and not only guarding our identities, but deeply internalizing our identities in Christ so that we do not fall victim to the enemy's thievery.

The only way to protect ourselves from spiritual identity theft is to study, absorb, accept, and believe what Scripture says about us and then refute the lies of the enemy with that truth. We must allow God's word, which is living and active and sharper than any two-edged sword, to completely and utterly transform us at our very core. This goes beyond equipping ourselves with mere information. I'm talking about a deeply personal knowing that only transpires when we spend regular time with the Lord in worship, prayer, and His word.

The One with whom we can completely entrust our wallet—our hearts—is Jesus. We desperately need God to flood our hearts with the truth about His radical love for us so that our identities are rock-solid. We can then powerfully and effectively guard our hearts. Then no one will ever be able to pilfer our purses.

Daily Prayer

Dear Lord,

I want to believe what Your word says about me, not how I might feel about myself. I long for a rock-solid identity. Please help me to truly understand who I am in Christ—my true identity as Your treasured daughter. Enable me to accept what Your word declares, that I am Your beloved, the apple of Your eye, and that I am precious to You.

Show me any lies I have believed so that I can replace them with the truth of Your word. Displace every lie, even those on a subconscious level, with Your truth and light, and help me never to trade my costly identity for the lies of the enemy again. Help me to not only understand but to genuinely internalize the reality of Your deep love for me, and let Your love be the anchor that firmly holds my identity in place. Flood my heart with Your love and enable me to experience Your presence in a very real way. Transform me, Lord, so that I am confident as Your daughter and so that my true identity in Jesus Christ can never be stolen. In the precious name of Jesus, amen.

God's Word for Me

I am more than a conqueror and gain a surpassing victory through Him who loves me (Romans 8:37 AMP).

I will not be foolish, but understand what the Lord's will is (Ephesians 5:17).

I will be strong in the Lord and in his mighty power (Ephesians 6:10).

I will walk by the Spirit, and I will not gratify the desires of the flesh (Galatians 5:16).

You will be a Father to me, and I will be your daughter (2 Corinthians 6:18).

I am being transformed into his image with ever-increasing glory, which comes from the Lord, who is the Spirit (2 Corinthians 3:18).

I accept others just as Christ has accepted me so that God will be given glory (Romans 15:7 NLT).

My Walk with God

Enoch has always fascinated me. Very little is mentioned about him in the Bible, but what *is* said is intriguing: "Enoch walked faithfully with God" (Genesis 5:22). I've spent a lot of years wondering what, exactly, it looked like for Enoch to walk with God. Was he a crazy-looking man who walked around muttering to himself—only it wasn't himself he was talking to, but God? Did he gaze at the stars in wonder, whispering to God of their beauty? Did Enoch chop wood, hunt game for dinner, and start fires in the wind...all while conversing with the Lord?

Verse 24 goes on to say "then he was no more, because God took him away." In other words, Enoch didn't die a natural death. Apparently Enoch's walk with God was so close, so in sync with what God was doing in and through him, that the Lord simply snatched the man up to heaven, allowing Enoch to skip the dying part.

Somehow, that makes me yearn to walk more closely with God too.

I try to imagine what it means to walk completely in tandem with God, our relationship so close that it could be said of me, "She walked with God." Some days find me talking to God in my car, in my closet, in the shower, and while I scrub pots at my kitchen sink. I speak to God when I arise in the morning, when I lay my head on my pillow each night, and when a bird sings sweetly outside my office window in the afternoon.

But some days I rush along, struggling to keep up with the demands of the day, and when evening falls I realize I've barely acknowledged Him at all. It's not as easy to walk as closely to God, I think, as it used to be. Many things compete for not only our attention, but our time…and our hearts. It's up to us to cultivate the yearning to be women who walk in habitual fellowship with God.

I once heard that we are each as close to God as we want to be. My fervent prayer is that we realize our proximity to the Lord is a choice we alone can make, one that we must choose every day. Choices soon become habit. And before we know it, we too can walk like Enoch walked—in intimate fellowship with God.

Daily Prayer

Dear Lord,

My heart's desire is to spend the time You have given me on this earth walking closely to You, completely in sync with Your will and plans and purpose for me each day. Please help me not to rush through my day without including You. Help me to regularly turn my thoughts toward You so that I don't unintentionally exclude You as I go about my day.

Capture my gaze, Lord, and overwhelm my heart with the reality of Your presence so that I find nothing more intriguing or beguiling than walking closely to You. Make Yourself real to me, and as I choose to draw near to You, I pray that You will draw near to me. Give me a heart that longs to remain near to You, longs to obey You, and longs to acknowledge You throughout every one of my days. You are the most important thing, Lord, and my desire is to walk in step with You every moment. In Jesus's precious name, amen.

God's Word for Me

I will dwell in the shelter of the Most High; I will rest in the shadow of the Almighty (Psalm 91:1).

I will come near to God and he will come near to me (James 4:8).

By day the LORD directs his love, at night his song is with me—a prayer to the God of my life (Psalm 42:8).

My whole being follows hard after You and clings closely to You, Your right hand upholds me (Psalm 63:8 AMP).

I will inquire of and for the Lord and crave Him and His strength; I will seek and require His face and His presence [continually] (Psalm 105:4 AMP).

My heart says of you, "Seek his face!" Your face, LORD, I will seek (Psalm 27:8).

Guide me in your truth and teach me, for you are God my Savior, and my hope is in you all day long (Psalm 25:5).

My Ability to Hear God's Voice

A fat lot of good those directions are doing me now!"
I shook my head as I drove down the interstate
toward the next town, wondering how on earth I was
going to find someone's house without their address,
street name, or a clue. Three weeks prior, my then
twelve-year-old son Josh had been invited to a birthday party with a phone call. Chatting with the birthday boy's mom, I wrote down the directions to their
home and taped them on the cupboard wall right next
to the phone so I wouldn't lose them. And there they
remained.

"What are we going to do, Mommy?" My six-year-
old daughter, Emily, stared out the window from her
booster seat. I had no idea.

As we turned down a road that I hoped led in the
right direction, I vaguely remembered the name of a
side street. Hopefully I'd recognize it with certainty
when and if I found it. I also trusted it would lead me
to the actual street the birthday boy lived on. My only
option was to pray, as I had neglected to bring along

the birthday boy's phone number—not my most brilliant move.

So, I prayed. Fervently. I drove and prayed, asking the Lord to *Please get us there,* since it was a 25-mile ride home and the party was about to begin. Frustration gripped me, but I pressed on. *Do we turn here, Lord? Or there?*

Ten minutes later, we all let out a hoot when we recognized the family's van and I pulled into their driveway. I opened my car door, stepped onto the driveway and shouted "God got us here! The Lord really got us here!" Somehow, in spite of no directions, no actual street name, and no GPS or smartphone (they didn't exist at the time), God enabled me to hear His voice. Incredible. And if I can discern God's voice through deep inner panic and crazy traffic, so can you.

It's tempting to think that we can't hear from God, especially when we're driving blind. But God's Word clearly tells us we *can* hear His voice. John 10:4 says that we know His voice. Verse 27 says "My sheep listen to my voice; I know them, and they follow me."

I have to chuckle when I catch myself asking God to speak clearly to me. I don't think God mumbles, and I do believe our hearing can be fine-tuned. We simply need ears to hear (see Matthew 11:15).

Two keys to hearing God's voice are to

(1) continually listen and (2) to get to know His voice. This requires ongoing practice to become familiar with the voice of the One who regularly speaks to our hearts. Then, just like we automatically hear and recognize the voice of a close friend when we answer the phone, we will always hear and recognize the Lord's voice when He speaks to us.

Daily Prayer

Father God,

I long to hear Your voice more clearly and more often. Please give me ears to hear what Your Spirit is saying to me, God, and help me to clearly recognize when You are speaking. Remove all doubt and confusion and enable me to hear and recognize Your voice, even in the midst of difficult, unsettling, or crazy circumstances. May Your voice ring true and clear in my heart, Oh God, and may I always have the ability through Your Holy Spirit to discern Your words to me. Thank You that I hear the voice of the Good Shepherd, and the voice of a stranger I will never follow. Lead and guide me daily as I turn my heart and my ears toward You, Lord. Give me a hunger and a passion for Your word so that I can more accurately recognize when You speak. In Jesus's name, amen.

God's Word for Me

Today, I will hear his voice and I will not harden my heart (Hebrews 3:15).

The voice of the LORD is powerful (Psalm 29:4).

I want to know Christ—yes, to know the power of his resurrection and participation in his sufferings, becoming like him in his death (Philippians 3:10).

I have ears; I will hear (Matthew 11:15).

I listen to the shepherd's voice; I know him, and I follow him (John 10:27).

I know that I have come to know him if I keep his commands (1 John 2:3).

I will listen to what God the LORD says; he promises peace to his people, his faithful servants (Psalm 85:8).

My Balance

My daily routine never varied: I dusted, vacuumed, tidied, and organized my entire house every single day. It took hours, but that didn't matter. I wanted a clean house, needed a clean house. My floors were immaculate, my kitchen countertops pristine. My bathrooms were so spotless that when a friend visited for the first time, she came out after washing her hands and said she felt embarrassed at how hers compared. My impeccable home made her feel uncomfortable, as though she could never measure up. That was the beginning of a wake-up call for me.

I was severely out of balance. A clean house meant more to me than it should have, and it placed pressure on me and my family. When I became aware of my need for a compulsively clean house, I began to pray and ask God to bring balance. Over the years He changed me, and I can honestly say that my house has truly never been compulsively spotless since.

Often our lives swing out of balance before we realize it. I'll be the first to raise my hand and confess I struggle to walk in balance when so many things compete for my attention. But here's something I've learned: We choose to respond to requirements, demands, and invitations every day.

Many things *require* my attention, such as my relationship with God, my relationship with my husband and family, relationships with friends, exercise, and my work. Many other things *demand* my attention, such as the laundry, housework, errands, cooking, pet care… the list goes on. And still other things *invite* my attention. These things are usually the least important but possess a powerful pull. They hold the potential to jerk me out of balance faster than anything else: Facebook and Twitter, fiction reading, and telephone calls.

But here's something I've learned. My *requirements* are non-negotiable. These hold the highest place in my priorities and unless there is some sort of crisis or emergency, they remain the most important and receive most of my attention.

I constantly juggle and shift my *demands*, accommodating each one on a fairly regular basis. (Laundry waits for no man, especially at my house.) But my *invitations*, which often hold the strongest pull, will yank me off track if I don't remember my goal to walk in balance. It's okay—even good—for me to accept some of those invitations; I just can't allow them to absorb all my time.

If we want to walk in balance, our choices should

mirror that desire. When we're willing to yield to the promptings of the Holy Spirit, our lives can swing from completely out of balance to manageable, and ultimately to flowing within the wise, healthy, productive parameters God desires.

Daily Prayer

Dear Lord,

Please forgive me for allowing myself to be pulled completely off track and out of balance at times. I know that You desire for me to walk in balance in every area of my life, and right now I make the commitment to discern between the requirements, the demands, and the invitations in my life. Help me to distinguish the difference between each and enable me to prioritize each area according to Your will.

Give me wisdom and grace to flow between the requirements, demands, and invitations in my life. Help me to resist the temptation to spend too much time in one area and neglect other areas. I also ask You, Lord, to help me walk in balance with my eating habits and exercise, with work and play, and in every area of my life. Give me grace and wisdom and the divine ability to be completely led by Your Holy Spirit

so that I can live a balanced life that is healthy, wise,
and pleasing to You. In Jesus's wonderful name, amen.

God's Word for Me

Teach me to do your will, for you are my God
(Psalm 143:10).

Let the morning bring me word of your unfailing
love, for I have put my trust in you. Show me the
way I should go, for to you I entrust my life
(Psalm 143:8).

Discretion will protect me, and understanding
will guard me (Proverbs 2:16).

I will be well balanced, vigilant, and cautious at all
times (1 Peter 5:8 AMP).

I will walk, live, and conduct myself in a manner
worthy of the Lord, desiring to please Him in all
things (Colossians 1:10 AMP).

His divine power has given me everything I need
for a godly life (2 Peter 1:3).

I will not turn to the right or the left; I will keep
my foot from evil (Proverbs 4:27).

My Weariness

I called her my Velcro-baby, because it seemed that between nursing and holding her, she was adhered to me. The precious baby girl for whom I had prayed cried incessantly—unless she was being held. My lower back had been injured while giving birth, preventing me from using a snuggie, so I held her with my left arm nearly all the time and became quite adept at accomplishing my daily tasks with one hand. But it cost me.

I cooked with one hand, vacuumed with one hand, and showered as fast as I could while she wailed with all her might. For six months I experienced physical weariness beyond what I thought myself capable of enduring.

At the same time, I was in the spiritual battle of my life. My relationship with my husband was at an all-time low. Sleep-deprived and hormonal, I longed for his comfort and help with the baby. But my husband was not at the place where he could offer me emotional encouragement or much help with the baby. I felt utterly overwhelmed.

A deep weariness seeped into my heart, and at midnight, I found myself curled up in a ball out on my driveway, sobbing. I was physically, emotionally, and spiritually depleted. I didn't think I could go on, and began to wonder why I should.

We all experience seasons of deep weariness at some point in our lives. Some seasons of weariness are short, but others last for what seems an unbearable length of time. It's then that serious discouragement can enter in. Elijah experienced a deep weariness after an amazing victory over the prophets of Baal (see 1 Kings, chapter 18). God knew Elijah would be physically, emotionally, and spiritually depleted, so He provided an oasis of supernatural encouragement—right when Elijah lay down in the desert and wanted to die.

God does the same for us. When we are overwhelmed by a battle that's gone on too long, when we've run a long, exhausting race, and when we are at the brink of utter despondency, God's divine provision is available to strengthen, encourage, and rejuvenate us. The Lord knows where we are, and He lovingly meets us right there with a cool drink of His Spirit and warm sustenance from heaven.

The next time weariness seeps into your bones, ask God to provide a supernatural oasis of encouragement to replenish, revive, and strengthen your soul.

Daily Prayer

Father,

You know what I'm enduring right now, and the deep weariness that threatens to choke out every morsel of strength I have left. I'm asking for Your divine provision in this place, Lord. I realize that apart from You I can do nothing, so I lean completely on You and ask You to infuse me with Your strength. Please rejuvenate me so that I do not grow weary in doing good.

If the joy of the Lord is my strength, then I ask that You pour down Your joy from heaven and strengthen me. Gird me with Your strength and fill and flood my heart with Your joy. Surround me with Your presence and lift my heart. Be my glory and the lifter of my head, God! Intervene in these circumstances of which I'm so weary, but if not, then like Shadrach, Meshach, and Abednego, accompany me while I'm in the fire. Thank You that I'm never alone, because You said You would always be with me. Draw near to me, God, so that I can draw my strength from You. Give me a fresh, accurate perspective, and encourage me by allowing me to see Your hand at work in my life. Thank You for Your faithfulness, Your goodness, and Your steadfast love. Thank You for being my supernatural oasis, my joy, and my strength. In the mighty name of Jesus, amen.

God's Word for Me

I will not become weary in doing good,
for at the proper time I will reap a harvest if I do
not give up (Galatians 6:9).

I will not grieve, for the joy of the LORD is my
strength (Nehemiah 8:10).

The LORD is my rock, my fortress and my deliverer; my God is my rock, in whom I take refuge, my shield and the horn of my salvation, my
stronghold (Psalm 18:2).

I have strength and joy, which are in your
dwelling place (1 Chronicles 16:27).

You have armed me with strength for the battle
(Psalm 18:39).

I will not become weary or lose heart, but will
continue in well-doing without weakening
(2 Thessalonians 3:13 AMP).

The LORD is my strength and my shield; my heart
trusts in him, and he helps me. My heart leaps for
joy, and with my song I praise him (Psalm 28:7).

My Perseverance

The ringing doorbell brought sheer relief to my soul. I hurried toward the front door, breathing a prayer of thanks. The cavalry had finally arrived. The peep-hole revealed two beaming women who enthusiastically sang out a joyful greeting when I opened the door. I took one look at their happy, well-rested faces and burst into tears.

Recognizing they obviously had not arrived to merely clean my house, but to offer postpartum counseling services, Glenda and Carol listened to my litany of complaints. "The baby never sleeps," I began. "She wants to be fed every hour and a half. If I put her down she just screams and screams." Shuddering breaths interrupted my words. "I...can't...even...eat...my... lunch...unless I'm holding her." Attempting to contain myself, I inhaled deeply. "I'm exhausted!" Hot tears poured down my face.

With my husband's blessing, I had arranged for my two friends to help with housework as I recuperated from the birth of our third child. Now these wonderful women stood before me, offering moral support to one sleep-starved, hormonal mom.

The next six months were some of the roughest I've ever walked through. I suffered major sleep deprivation along with depression which stemmed from serious anemia and thyroid issues. To add insult to injury, I experienced a painful bout of (ahem!) hemorrhoids so severe that surgery was required—just seven days postpartum. Everything in me just wanted to lie down and give up.

Each one of us will have to persevere through unpleasant circumstances at some point in our lives. Whether it's financial, physical, relational or personal, tenacity is not optional. The temptation to quit can feel powerfully alluring and appealing. Yet Hebrews 10:36 tells us "You need to persevere so that when you have done the will of God, you will receive what he has promised."

Starting something is easy. But finishing that thing, persevering until the end, is what really matters. Ecclesiastes 7:8 reminds us "The end of a matter is better than the beginning." We can only do this by making the choice to keep going through the power of the Holy Spirit.

Perseverance is always a choice. When we refuse to give up, when we make the decision to press on in

Christ's strength and endure, we will always come out on the other end stronger, wiser, and ultimately enjoying God's promises.

Daily Prayer

Father God,

Please grant me a willing, persevering heart. Help me not to give up or grow weary in doing good. Strengthen me so that I can continue to move forward into all that You have for me. Help me not to give up or let go of the promises You've given me. Help me not to allow myself to be lazy or to entertain tempting thoughts about quitting. Right now in the name of Jesus I determine to press on no matter how difficult things become. Thank You for Your grace and Your strength that enable me to press forward.

Thank You for the joy of the Lord, which is my strength and enables me to stand and keep standing. Help me to never stop believing that You are at work in my situation. Enable me to persevere in every circumstance and bring You glory. Grant me steadfast patience and endurance so that I can perform and fully accomplish Your will, and then receive what You have promised. In Jesus's name, amen.

God's Word for Me

I glory in my sufferings, because I know that suffering produces perseverance in me (Romans 5:3).

I pray that I will be strengthened with all power according to his glorious might so that I may have great endurance and patience (Colossians 1:11).

I will be mature and complete, not lacking anything (James 1:4).

I will watch out that I do not lose what I have worked for, that I may be rewarded fully (2 John 1:8).

I will stand firm to the end (Matthew 10:22).

I honor those who fear the LORD; I keep an oath even when it hurts, and do not change my mind (Psalm 15:4).

I will put on the full armor of God, so that when the day of evil comes, I may be able to stand my ground (Ephesians 6:13).

My Worship

It was as if a thick, warm blanket enveloped me. I knelt, allowing the microphone in my hand to slide onto the carpet. God's magnificent presence so overwhelmed me I could not sing. I could only kneel—and tremble. Awestruck, I basked in what felt like intense rays of love. Eventually, the praise and worship portion of our Sunday morning church service was over, and I took my seat in the sanctuary along with the rest of the worship team.

Most of us think the above scenario is what worship looks and feels like, but as wonderful as that moment was, the truth is we can worship God and experience His presence absolutely anywhere. Whether we're standing at the kitchen sink or walking through the grocery store, we can worship the Lord. Whether we're folding laundry or giving our children (or grandchildren) a bath, we can worship Him.

Jesus said that those who worship will worship in Spirit and in Truth. And since every believer has the Spirit of God living inside them, and Jesus is Truth, beautiful moments of worship can spontaneously erupt out of us regardless of our location—or situation.

One of the most powerful moments to worship the Lord is probably one that makes the least sense: when we're enduring particularly difficult circumstances or when we simply don't feel like it. If your flesh is anything like mine, depending on the day, sometimes the last thing I'm inclined to do is turn on a hallelujah chorus and sing along. Perhaps that's why Scripture admonishes us to bring the Lord a sacrifice of praise (see Hebrews 13:15). Because sometimes, worship will truly cost us.

An attitude of worship is more than merely singing songs—it's turning our hearts, our focus, and our attention towards our holy, awesome God, and telling Him through a whisper, a thought, a song, or a dance, that we love and adore Him.

It's so easy to worship when our needs are met, when we are comfortable, happy, and the world is right. But true worship happens in the most unlikely places and times. As we dare to abandon ourselves in true worship at inconvenient times or when our emotions are demanding a pity party, our hearts will become enraptured by the One who loves us most. And *that* is true worship.

Daily Prayer

Dear Lord,

Grant me a worshipping heart, one that recognizes and praises You for all You are and for all You've done. Help me to recognize Your hand at work in my life and honor You through regular, authentic, spontaneous worship. Give me the ability to worship You even in difficult times. May my focus never stray from You. May no circumstance, situation, or person ever capture my gaze like You do. And even when it's hard, help me choose to look away from all that distracts unto Jesus. Help me to keep my focus on You.

Enable me to choose to worship You even when it feels inconvenient or my emotions aren't 100 percent there. May my heart praise and worship You in spirit and in truth throughout each day. Help me to worship You with abandon and become a woman after Your own heart. Captivate my heart, Lord, as I worship You. Make Yourself real to me and allow me to sense Your presence through worship. In the precious name of Jesus, amen.

God's Word for Me

God is spirit, and I will worship Him in Spirit and in truth (John 4:24).

The reverent fear and worship of the Lord is my treasure and His (Isaiah 33:6).

Show me your ways, LORD, teach me your paths. Guide me in your truth and teach me, for you are God my Savior, and my hope is in you all day long (Psalm 25:4-5).

I will ascribe to the LORD the glory due his name; I will worship the LORD in the splendor of his holiness (Psalm 29:2).

With my mouth I will greatly extol the LORD (Psalm 109:30).

I will exalt the LORD our God and worship at his holy mountain, for the LORD our God is holy (Psalm 99:9).

I thank God when I worship with a clear conscience (2 Timothy 1:3).

My Strength

They were only words, yet they wounded like a venomous snakebite. And though I chose to forgive, my heart hurt so badly I couldn't get it together to do all I had planned that day. In fact, the emotional strain left me feeling drained and completely weak, as if I had no strength. I completely related to King David, who said "My strength is dried up like a fragment of clay pottery" (Psalm 22:15 AMP).

It's not easy to continue on when our strength is depleted. No one knows that like Jesus. He endured rejection, painful taunts, and the ever-present challenges of the Pharisees. But Jesus knew the secret to His strength lay not in a life free of hurtful words, pressing deadlines, and daily distresses, but in spending time with His Father. God alone held the ability to replenish and revive Him.

Sometimes, instead of doggedly pressing on through exhaustion, we need to rest and allow God's presence to resuscitate our drained hearts and souls. As we wait on the Lord, our strength will be renewed like the eagle's. We will run and not grow weary; we will walk and will not faint (Isaiah 40:31).

So instead of jumping into the shower first thing on that particular morning, I decided to spend time relaxing with worship music and Jesus. I curled up on some throw pillows and allowed gentle waves of worship music to cascade over me, soothing my heart and emotions. I cried, I sang, and I poured out my heart to Jesus. Soon His comforting presence enveloped me and I could feel my strength slowly returning. Though my day was still difficult, God's grace lifted me.

Life can be hard, and sometimes it takes more out of us than we have left. Yet God says, "My grace is all you need. My power works best in weakness" (2 Corinthians 12:9 NLT). When we take time to rest in God's presence and accept God's grace, we can begin to move forward in God's strength.

Even the most resilient of us experiences feeble and frail moments—we're human. The truth is, apart from Jesus, we have no strength to count on, and we cannot accomplish anything. But when we spend time with Him, He refreshes, revives, and strengthens us. Jesus is our only reliable source of strength, and He graciously imparts it to us when we make time for Him and ask.

Daily Prayer

Oh God,

There are times when absolutely all strength leaves me, and I feel drained, depleted, and utterly weak. It's then that I feel I cannot go on. Please help me to remember that You are my source of strength, Jesus. When I have no strength, give me grace to simply come to You and allow You to fill me and gird me with Your strength.

But God, I also realize You work best in my weakness. And I know I am always weak, whether I realize it in the moment or not. Since Your power works best in my weakness, I pray You will accomplish Your will and plan and purpose in my weak moments. I ask You to touch others, work through me, and demonstrate Your power and lovingkindness through my weakness. Lord, I turn to You, realizing that You alone have the ability to refresh, revive, and restore my strength. Please help me to rest in You, receive my strength from You, and continue on in Your strength. In Jesus's name, amen.

God's Word for Me

I will trust in the Lord and find new strength.
I will run and not grow weary,
I will walk and not faint
(Isaiah 40:31 NLT).

I can do all this through him who gives me
strength (Philippians 4:13).

I will boast all the more gladly about my weaknesses, so that Christ's power may rest on me
(2 Corinthians 12:9).

I will not grieve, for the joy of the LORD
is my strength (Nehemiah 8:10).

You are my strength, I sing praise to you; you,
God, are my fortress, my God on whom I can rely
(Psalm 59:17).

The LORD is my strength and my shield; my heart
trusts in him, and he helps me. My heart leaps for
joy, and with my song I praise him (Psalm 28:7).

For Christ's sake, I delight in weaknesses, in
insults, in hardships, in persecutions, in difficulties. For when I am weak, then I am strong
(2 Corinthians 12:10).

My Decisions

Making decisions was always challenging for me. An insecure, peace-craving people-pleaser most of my life, I grew up without really being in touch with my own preferences, so decision making was especially hard. As I matured spiritually and began walking in more freedom, I began taking back the abilities I had abdicated as a young girl, and then I was faced with figuring out how well-made decisions unfold.

Thank God for Colossians 3:15 (AMP), which, to my surprise, embedded the picture of a professional baseball game in my mind, igniting my heart with an understanding of how God works and leads us when we're making decisions. "And let the peace (soul harmony which comes) from Christ rule (act as umpire continually) in your hearts [deciding and settling with finality all questions that arise in your minds, in that peaceful state] to which as [members of Christ's] one body you were also called [to live]. And be thankful."

We've all watched at least one umpire in action at a baseball game. Both teams and the audience look to the umpire for the official decision on close plays. The umpire's decision is not always liked, or agreed with, but it is always clear, and it's always final.

As we approach any decision, we should always begin by asking Jesus, the Umpire in our lives, for wisdom and clear direction. We can then resist pressure or rushing into a decision, because "To be overhasty is to sin and miss the mark" (Proverbs 19:2 AMP). Then we can do our best to follow after peace.

Decisions can still produce a tug-of-war in our hearts and minds—after all, we want to take our decisions seriously and don't want to miss God's direction. But when we allow our decisions to be led by peace, we're actually discerning the Prince of Peace's will in our lives. That soul harmony referenced in Colossians 3:15 clearly indicates that we are on the right track.

Though making decisions is not always easy, God knows our hearts. He knows we want His guidance in our decisions, and ultimately, He understands our desire to honor and obey Him. So when we begin to struggle, we can remember that God will (eventually) make His will clear to us. He will prevent us from going the wrong way. And if somehow we unintentionally go the wrong way, He will gently usher us back onto the right path.

As we attempt to make decisions, we can trust God to guide us and give us wisdom when we ask Him; He will lead us according to His will, His plan, and His purpose.

Daily Prayer

Father God,

I desire for Your will to be established in all of my decision making, in decisions both small and great. Right now I yield my desires and preferences to You, because being in the center of Your will matters more to me than the direction or outcome of the decisions I'm making. I choose to acknowledge You, Father. According to Your word, make my paths straight.

I ask for You to cause my thoughts to become agreeable to Your will, and then my plans will be established and succeed. Guide and direct me by the power of Your Holy Spirit. Lord, give me clarity and direction as I think through the options before me. Please enable me to follow after peace. Help me not to move forward when I sense frustration or uncertainty, but enable me to pause until Your peace shows me the way. Give me wisdom, clarity, and direction as I look to You for help in all my decision making. In Jesus's name, amen.

God's Word for Me

I will trust in the Lord with all my heart and will not lean on my own understanding (Proverbs 3:5).

In all my ways I will submit to him, and he will make my paths straight (Proverbs 3:6).

I will give careful thought to the paths for my feet and be steadfast in all my ways (Proverbs 4:26).

In my heart I plan my course, but the Lord establishes my steps (Proverbs 16:9).

When I lack wisdom I will ask God, who gives generously (James 1:5).

You have lavished on me every kind of wisdom
and understanding, practical insight
and prudence (Ephesians 1:18 AMP).

I have the wisdom from above and I am willing
to yield to reason (James 3:17 AMP).

My Expectations

My expectations always seemed to trip me up. I expected life to be easy. I expected a conflict-free marriage. I expected my prayers to be answered ASAP, with no regard to God's timing or the Holy Spirit's tender wooing. And I placed unrealistically high expectations on myself to do everything right. No wonder I walked around feeling frustrated so much of the time.

There is a vast difference between faith-filled watching, which keeps us in God's peace as He works, and a demanding sort of expectation, which creates frustration in our hearts when the expectation is not met. Faith believes, but expectations demand. After years of dashed expectations, God finally showed me that my expectations were often selfish desires in disguise.

And while God does want us to expect Him to move in our hearts, lives, and situations, there is a huge difference between a holy expectation born of faith and placing our expectations on the people or circumstances involved—or even on ourselves. Expectations placed anywhere but on Jesus usually lead to pressure, stress, and frustration.

Some expectations are legitimate, some are unrealistic. Expecting a chair to support my weight when I sit down is a reasonable expectation. Expecting my two-year-old granddaughter not to wail in the grocery store is my wish, but given her age, probably not a realistic expectation.

Discerning between the two isn't always so clear-cut. So how do we walk a healthy balance between expecting God to move in faith and the reality of disappointments, setbacks, and unfulfilled desires? These three things will help:

Faith. A mature faith understands and believes God is at work in spite of how things might appear. Authentic faith is a deep trust that God orchestrates our lives and can accomplish the seemingly impossible.

A submissive heart. When we reverently accept God's sovereign plan and timing, we demonstrate and acknowledge that He is in control, not us. Genuine submission also releases us from the pressure of unrealistic expectations.

Focus. The willingness and ability to place—and keep—our expectations exclusively on the Lord prevents us from placing pressure on others. We're free to authentically accept people where they are when our eyes are on the Lord.

When we walk in faith with a submissive heart, keeping our focus on Jesus, we demonstrate trust in the One whose timing, plans, and purposes are perfect.

Daily Prayer

Lord,

I don't want my expectations to trip me up. I ask You to enable me to discern the difference in my heart between faith-filled expectation and my own unrealistic expectations.

Please help me to have realistic expectations for myself and those around me. Help me not to frustrate my family members and friends with unrealistic, selfish expectations. Please forgive me for any demanding tones in my heart, and for insisting on my own way, placing pressure on myself and others. Give me the grace to willingly submit my desires and plans to You, reverently accepting Your sovereign plan and timing because not only do I have faith in You, but I trust You, Lord. Help me to keep my focus on You, Father, and then my expectations will not be disappointed. I will wait and hope for and expect You, Lord. I will wait patiently, expecting and looking for You. In Jesus's name, amen.

God's Word for Me

I will wait for the Lord; I will be strong and take heart and wait for the Lord (Psalm 27:14).

But now, Lord, what do I look for?
My hope is in you (Psalm 39:7).

I will keep myself in God's love as I wait for the mercy of our Lord Jesus Christ to bring me to eternal life (Jude 1:21).

I will expect, look for, and hope in Him and my strength will be renewed (Isaiah 40:31 AMP).

May integrity and uprightness protect me, because my hope, Lord, is in you (Psalm 25:21).

Yes, my soul, find rest in God; my hope comes from him (Psalm 62:5).

The Lord expect and longs to be gracious to me; therefore he will rise up to show me compassion (Isaiah 30:18).

My Disqualified Feelings

There was a time when I thought God couldn't possibly use me. Between my rough childhood, my shameful past, and my miserable marriage, I could not imagine a less likely candidate.

My heart was calling me to believe God, to run with passion the race I sensed Him calling me toward. But at the same time, vestiges from my past would flash in my mind, or I'd react wrongly to a situation and feel ashamed, or a relational conflict would erupt, and I no longer felt able to pursue my passion. One day I felt confident of my calling, and the next day I felt utterly disqualified.

Can you relate? Feeling disqualified crushes our ability to move forward. But we can take heart that God's perspective is vastly different from ours, and He sees us differently from the way we see ourselves. We can begin to rise above feeling disqualified and come into agreement with God's plans and purposes for us when we consider the following:

First, God's love never fails. It's His love in us that qualifies us, transforms us, and works in and through us. Even in our hardest moments, God's love lifts us, enables us, and compels us to keep running.

Second, God's gifts and callings are irrevocable. God knew the hurts I would endure and the mistakes I would make. He knows our shortcomings. But His specific calling on our lives does not disintegrate the moment we fail or doubt. This does not give us license to sin, or excuse us from pursuing godly character. On the contrary, it should instill a desire to become more Christ-like so we can pursue our race with confidence.

Third, He uses our scars. Our past is not a bashing tool in the enemy's hand. Our unique experiences, coupled with God's healing power and grace, equip us to minister God's comfort, truth, and healing to others who have experienced the same wounds. God never wastes our pain.

Finally, it's a process. We are all in the process of becoming more like Jesus. As we press forward, it is wise to remember that God is not finished with us yet, and He will complete the good work He has begun in us.

Years ago I read a powerfully inspiring book called *Eric Liddell: Something Greater Than Gold*. It's the story of a gifted young Scottish athlete who trained to run in the 1924 Olympics. In my favorite chapter, Eric is running his event when on the final lap another runner knocks him down. Assuming he is disqualified from the race, Eric lies on the ground on the sidelines, anguished at the loss of his shot at an Olympic gold medal.

When he finally looks up, Eric sees his coach frantically motioning for him to get up and get back into the race. Stunned, Eric realizes he is not disqualified after all. Jumping up, he determines to run his best race, in spite of the lost time. The audience roars as Eric begins passing the other runners, and to everyone's surprise, he wins the gold medal.

The enemy would love for us to believe that we are disqualified and our race is over. But if we will dare to look up, our Ultimate Coach—Jesus—is fervently cheering us on. He sees our efforts, He's encouraging us to stay in the race, and He cannot wait for us to cross the finish line. Being knocked down does not disqualify us. We must simply choose to get back up and keep running.

Daily Prayer

Father,

When my past memories or present circumstances threaten to overwhelm me and it feels like I've been knocked out of the race, help me to remember that You have plans for my hope, plans for my good and for my future. Please forgive me for allowing myself to feel disqualified when it is by Jesus's blood alone that I am found acceptable in Your sight.

You say in Your word that I should not let anyone defraud me by acting as an umpire and declaring me unworthy and disqualifying me for the prize. So I will choose not to listen to the voice of doubt or the lies of the enemy. Instead, I will choose to believe that I can do all things through Christ who strengthens me. Help me not to trip over feeling disqualified, but instead enable me to run with passion the race I sense You calling me toward. Strengthen and equip me to finish my race with joy. In Jesus's name, amen.

God's Word for Me

I will not let anyone defraud me and declare me unworthy, disqualifying me for the prize (Colossians 2:18 AMP).

I press on toward the goal to win the prize for which God has called me heavenward in Christ Jesus (Philippians 3:14).

I can do all this through him who gives me strength (Philippians 4:13).

You, Lord, have plans for me—plans to prosper me and not harm me, plans to give me a hope and a future (Jeremiah 29:11).

I have received power, ability and efficiency because the Holy Spirit has come upon me (Acts 1:8 AMP).

Not that I am competent in myself to claim anything for myself, but my competence comes from God (2 Corinthians 3:5).

For it is God who works in me to will and to act in order to fulfill his good purpose (Philippians 2:13).

My Security

I lay awake in my bed, uneasy. Though our house was quiet and peaceful, I sure wasn't. After several peeping-Tom incidents and two scary break-in attempts early in my life, nighttime was still difficult for me, even years later. As I glanced up toward our security system's keypad, I saw the little red light indicating that the house alarm was activated and all was well. I breathed a sigh of relief.

That's when I sensed God's gentle words. *Your alarm system is not what keeps you safe, Julie. I keep you safe. Even if your alarm system malfunctions, I will never fail you.* I closed my eyes and knew the Lord was right.

Sometimes past experiences leave such a strong indentation in our hearts, we unknowingly seek other forms of security besides God. But He wants to be our primary fortress—the One we run to for comfort and security first, not as an afterthought. Though our world is a scary place—just watching the news or glancing at a newspaper often makes me cringe—we can still know and experience the peace that passes all understanding.

King David experienced plenty of insecurity in his life. People's opinions of him shifted and changed. Many times he was laughed at, wished dead, and belittled. Yet David had a firm grasp of where his security lay. "Keep me safe, my God, for in you I take refuge" (Psalm 16:1).

In spite of frequently fierce opposition, David knew the Lord intimately and experienced a deep security so that even in the midst of troubling times he could sing. He proclaimed, "The LORD is my strength and my shield; my heart trusts in him, and he helps me. My heart leaps for joy, and with my song I praise him" (Psalm 28:7).

God wants to be so real to us that His presence overwhelms, reduces, and eventually displaces the negative memories and experiences that might cause us to feel insecure. He wants us to know Him as our refuge, our hiding place, and our strong tower.

Daily Prayer

Lord,

As a child longs for the security of her blankie, I long for Your comforting presence. When I feel insecure, remind me of Your strength and nearness. Thank You for being my ever-present help in every situation. Please wipe away any emotional residue from my past that makes me feel insecure. Be my inner strength and help me to consistently stand secure in You. When everything around me begins to feel shaky and unsettled and uncertain, I will remember that You are my stronghold and security. You are stronger than every opposing force, and I take comfort in knowing with confidence that You are always near me.

Thank You, Lord, that I have peace, righteousness, security, and triumph over opposition as my heritage as a servant of the Lord. I will say along with the Psalmist, in You I have found refuge, and in You do I put my trust and hide myself. In Jesus's name, amen.

God's Word for Me

Lord, you are the God who saves me; day and night I cry out to you (Psalm 88:1).

No weapon formed against me will prevail, and I will refute every tongue that accuses me (Isaiah 54:17).

Keep me safe, my God, for in you I take refuge
(Psalm 16:1).

I dwell in the shelter of the Most High and will
rest in the shadow of the Almighty (Psalm 91:1).

Never will you leave me; never will you forsake
me (Hebrews 13:5).

You are my strength, I sing praise to you; you,
God, are my fortress, my God on whom I can rely
(Psalm 59:17).

Truly he is my rock and my salvation; he is my
fortress, I will never be shaken (Psalm 62:2).

My Guilt

For too many years I walked around with a vague sense of guilt. I'd mess up, think wrong thoughts, or act inappropriately, and then feel guilty about it for days. I knew that my guilty feelings weren't helping me, but I felt helpless to change the pattern and escape the dreaded, ever-present guilt pangs. It's not that I wanted to feel guilty; I simply couldn't figure out how to *not* feel guilty.

Guilt acts like an imposing concrete barrier between us and God. Guilt points its condemning finger at us, accusing us of what we clearly already know. Yes, the Holy Spirit convicts us. But it's a gentle conviction that leads to life, not a condemning, hopeless, don't-you-ever-approach-me-again sense of unshakable guilt.

The difference is that the conviction of the Holy Spirit gently leads us toward God. The Spirit leads us to repentance and joy, teaches us, and enables us to sense His lovingkindness in the conviction. Guilt steers us away from God. It magnifies our issues and shrinks God's grace and forgiveness to microscopic concepts that seem far, far away.

Part of my guilt issue resulted because I would agree with the guilt. I mean, I always know when I mess up. But agreement with the guilt essentially crippled my heart. Yet God's grace and forgiveness are greater—even greater than the searing pain of a guilty heart. First John 3:20 says "If our hearts condemn us, we know that God is greater than our hearts, and he knows everything." What an awesome truth! God is greater than my guilty heart.

So now, whenever my heart feels the first twinges of guilt, I immediately pray. Perhaps my conscience is letting me know something is wrong, and I'm sensing the conviction of the Holy Spirit. In that case, I confess my sin and receive Christ's forgiveness, then move on. If a nagging sense of guilt remains, I know it's not from my heavenly Father—and I refuse to entertain it.

Part of successfully resisting and breaking free from an unhealthy guilt pattern is getting to know God's character more intimately. As we spend time getting to know the Lord through reading His word, prayer, and worship, we will begin to truly know His character. I've learned that God doesn't hold grudges. He isn't angry at me. His grace is sufficient. The more our wrong concepts are replaced by the truth of God's character and the supreme beauty of His gracious, loving character, the more we will walk in freedom from guilt.

Daily Prayer

Heavenly Father,

I'm so grateful that I don't have to feel weighed down with guilt, even when my heart agrees with it. Thank You for Your life-giving conviction, Lord, which leads me to repentance. Thank You that when I confess my sins, You are faithful and just to forgive me and cleanse me of all unrighteousness. Right now I ask You to reveal any unconfessed sin in my life so that my heart can be clean and free. Help me to always be sensitive to the conviction of Your Holy Spirit, and quick to repent of any sin.

Help me to grow to know You more intimately, because I know that as I understand Your character, I will be less inclined to indulge a guilty heart. It's not what You require of me, and I will not require it of myself. Thank You for freedom, for forgiveness, and for enabling me to successfully and permanently break free from walking in guilt. In Jesus's mighty name, amen.

God's Word for Me

The LORD is gracious and compassionate, slow to
anger and rich in love (Psalm 145:8).

As I live and walk in the light, I have fellowship
with others and the blood of Jesus Christ
cleanses me from all sin and guilt
(1 John 1:7 AMP).

But I, by your great love, can come into your
house; in reverence I bow down toward your holy
temple (Psalm 5:7).

But who can discern their own errors?
Forgive my hidden faults (Psalm 19:12).

My heart leaps for joy, and with my song I praise
him (Psalm 28:7).

My God comforts, encourages, and strengthens
my heart, keeping me unswerving in
every good work (2 Thessalonians 2:19 AMP).

I am overwhelmed with joy for He has dressed me
with salvation and draped me with a robe
of righteousness (Isaiah 61:10 AMP).

My Focus

When the phone rang that morning, I groaned. Writing deadlines and a to-do list as long as my driveway would have to wait. My daughter's parent-partnered school needed me, and since I was the parent on call, I'd be spending the day working at her school instead of accomplishing my goals. All day long I was tempted to think of everything I wasn't getting done at home. I was tempted to focus on my interrupted plans instead of focusing on being a blessing.

It's so easy to do. Sometimes I will actually focus on the one negative thing that happens to me in a day instead of the dozens of good things I experience. My thoughts sometimes resemble rain, flowing straight down to the lowest point. As my day continues, it's as if that single incident is a bright orange flag wildly waving on the periphery of my vision. Eventually my gaze is completely captured by that one negative thing.

But it doesn't have to be this way. When we focus on the negative, we become sidetracked. And if we risk becoming what we focus on, well, heaven help us. By focusing on a particular negative event we may think we're doing the right thing, but we're actually being distracted. When our gaze is taken away from the Lord, so is our peace.

Psalm 121:1-2 says "I lift up my eyes to the mountains—where does my help come from? My help comes from the LORD, the Maker of heaven and earth." Our help does not come from psychoanalyzing and focusing on the problem and stressing out. This may be the world's way of doing things, but as women of God we must *choose* for our primary focus to be the Lord and His voice.

When we become consumed with an issue, a person, or a circumstance, we risk losing perspective. We inadvertently magnify that thing and unintentionally shrink Jesus. We end up focused on our situation instead of the One who orders our steps and gives us grace.

Jesus will help us shift our focus from the overwhelming circumstances to Him—if we ask. Just as we sometimes stoop down and gently take our young child's chin in our hand and whisper "Look at me," the Lord wants to capture our complete attention by capturing our chin—and our heart—with His gaze. Isaiah

26:3 tells us, "You will keep in perfect peace those whose minds are steadfast, because they trust in you."

When a hard situation or our long to-do list keeps coming to our mind, we don't have to allow it to become our main focus. Instead, we can choose to glance at the facts while locking eyes with Jesus. When our focus is on Him, we will have perfect peace. Jesus is whispering *Look at Me.* He longs—and deserves to be—the center of our focus.

Daily Prayer

Dear Lord,

I desire to honor You in every area of my life, and I desire for You to be the center of my focus at all times, even when other things compete for my attention. Please touch my heart and draw me to You and help me to keep You front and center in my life. When I'm tempted to focus on the negative events that occur in my day, help me to remain grateful and not replay the negative over and over. Enable me to keep things in perspective and shift my focus to You. God, Your word says that You will keep in perfect peace him whose mind is fixed on You, so today I'm going to choose to focus and fix my mind on You. Your word also says that love pays no attention to a suffered wrong. So when the wrongs come, I'm going to choose to forgive, let it go, and move on, keeping You, Jesus, as my focus. Amen.

God's Word for Me

My heart has heard you say, "Come and talk with me." And my heart responds, "Lord, I am coming" (Psalm 27:8 NLT).

I will be still, and know that you are God (Psalm 46:10).

I will praise you, LORD, among the nations; I will sing of you among the peoples (Psalm 57:9).

You took me from my mother's womb and You have been my benefactor from that day (Psalm 71:6 AMP).

But as for me, it is good to be near God. I have made the Sovereign LORD my refuge (Psalm 73:28).

He alone is my rock and salvation, my fortress
where I will never be shaken
(Psalm 62:2 AMP).

I will look to the LORD and his strength; I will
seek his face always (Psalm 105:4).

My Plans

I admit it: I love an organized, tidy life. I prefer everything unfolding according to plan…a sensible, easy-going plan, that is. Unfortunately, life doesn't work that way. And frankly, some days I'd be happy just to *know* the plan.

You'd think that the One who created the Earth according to His extraordinary master plan would be delighted to drop freshly crafted blueprints into our hands so we could figure out where we're going in life and precisely how to get there. Yet God continually surprises me. And by that I mean things rarely go the way I expect, even when I think I'm keeping my expectations in check. God is far more interested in teaching us to hear His voice than making our plans unfold flawlessly.

It's good to trust God—to prayerfully believe in faith that He is going to move. But sometimes our idealistic plans morph into assumptions about God and what He is going to do in our lives, and that, my friends can be foolish ground.

As we're told in James 4:13-15, "Now listen, you

who say, 'Today or tomorrow we will go to this or that city, spend a year there, carry on business and make money.' Why, you do not even know what will happen tomorrow. What is your life? You are a mist that appears for a little while and then vanishes. Instead, you ought to say, 'If it is the Lord's will, we will live and do this or that.'"

Thankfully, God does not require us to perpetually walk in the dark and never have a clue about situations or our future (though sometimes it feels like it). Things don't always go according to our plans, yet sometimes God graciously allows us to catch glimpses of *His* plans. Yes, we walk by faith. But as we prayerfully submit our potential plans and the desires of our hearts to Him, He will lead and guide us. And the truth is, God can show us His plans if and when He desires, as we see clearly in the following Scripture: "But when he, the Spirit of truth, comes, he will guide you into all the truth. He will not speak on his own; he will speak only what he hears, and he will tell you what is yet to come" (John 16:13).

I'm grateful when God impresses on my heart the things that are to come. But if Jesus is our Lord, then He is sovereign over our plans, regardless of whether He reveals them to us or not. I think the best plan to follow is this: "Trust in the LORD with all your heart and lean not on your own understanding" (Proverbs 3:5).

Daily Prayer

Dear Lord,

As much as I sometimes desire and enjoy planning out different events and dreams, frequently down to the last detail, I much more desire for You to orchestrate everything. I know there is wisdom and protection when I submit to Your will in every area of my life. So right now, in the best way I know how, I relinquish all of my plans to You, and I ask You to cause my thoughts to become agreeable to Your will, and then my plans will be established and succeed.

I trust You to accomplish Your will and Your plan in my life. Help me not to become so attached to my plans and ideas that I become inflexible to the leading of Your Holy Spirit. May my plans never mean more to me than pleasing You and following Your plans for every situation in my life. Enable me to yield my desires, my hopes, and my control issues to You with a good attitude. Your word says that a man's mind plans his way, but the Lord directs his steps and makes them sure. So as my mind plans, Father, please direct my steps, make them sure, and be Lord over all my plans. In Jesus's name, amen.

God's Word for Me

I will praise the LORD, who counsels me; even at night my heart instructs me (Psalms 16:7).

Show me your ways, LORD, teach me your paths. Guide me in your truth and teach me, for you are God my Savior, and my hope is in you all day long (Psalm 25:4-5).

I will commit my way to the Lord; I will trust in him (Psalm 37:5).

Whether I turn to the right or to the left, my ears will hear a voice behind me, saying, "This is the way; walk in it" (Isaiah 30:21).

I will ask where the good way is, and walk in it (Jeremiah 6:16).

I have plans, but from the Lord comes the proper answer (Proverbs 16:1).

I will cry out to God Most High, to God, who will fulfill his purpose for me (Psalm 57:2 NLT).

My Contentment

I loathed my daily walks in Florida's unbearable summer heat and humidity. My exercise sessions felt more like torturous endurance sentences than a stroll around the block, and they left me overheated, dripping wet, and possibly even slightly cranky. My walks in the oppressive outdoor temperatures inevitably ended with me groaning and complaining about how unbearable it all was.

So as I sat on the floor listening to Joyce Meyer explain that just like the Israelites who wandered in the desert for 40 years, when we complain we remain, I was stunned. It never occurred to me that my complaining kept me exactly where I didn't want to be— in the Sauna State. I suddenly understood that unless I learned to be content right where I was, I'd *never* get to leave the boiling heat and live further north, and at the time, I desperately wanted to move north. While that might not be the most sincere motive, it was the beginning of my journey toward contentment.

I also began to realize that when my children complain and moan about what they already have, it made me not want to give them anything else—it would likely just end up being complained about at some point too. Was I guilty of this flagrant lack of gratitude as well?

Contentment is a treasure in today's culture, and we nurture it through intentional gratitude. Contentment protects us in a material world gone mad and enables us to stand against the excess of our society. Where the lust of the eyes desires more, more, more, wise contentment blissfully responds, "No thank you." When insatiable desire tries to pull us into debt, thankful contentment restrains us from purchases we cannot afford. When a roving eye gazes at another, grateful contentment is well pleased with the spouse we have.

Contentment graciously submits to God's sovereignty, trusting Him to place what He desires into our hands. It's not that we can't desire change or work towards obtaining necessary things. Rather, it's simply that we aren't controlled by the desire for more, better, or different.

It has been my experience that when I'm praying for a particular thing, God often waits to grant it until I'm grateful with what I have. This makes me realize I can truly be content either way before He answers. The Lord doesn't want us to desire any *thing* more than we desire Him. And we're much better off not having unchecked desires constantly gnawing at our hearts and minds.

A simple yet powerful way to cultivate contentment is through verbally expressing gratitude—regularly—to God and to others. Contentment is powerful warfare, and a sure protection against greed and dissatisfaction of every kind.

Daily Prayer

Dear Lord,

Your word says "godliness with contentment is great gain." Help me to practice contentment by cultivating a grateful heart. Open my eyes to the many blessings I have, and help me to continually remember to thank You for the many good things with which You've abundantly blessed me. When I'm not satisfied, help me to honor You by maintaining a godly attitude without complaining. Your word says to do all things without complaining, and I don't want to grieve Your Holy Spirit. Help me to remember that things cannot satisfy me, and that only You are capable of giving me true, lasting contentment. When I long and hope for change, whether it's a situation, a relationship, or a change in me, enable me to remain contented while I trust Your plan and Your timing for my life. Help me to walk in peaceful contentment every day of my life. In Jesus's name, amen.

God's Word for Me

I have God's peace, which exceeds anything I can understand. His peace will guard my heart and my mind in Christ Jesus (Philippians 4:7 NLT).

If I have food and clothing, I will be content with that (1 Timothy 6:8).

Godliness with contentment is great gain (1 Timothy 6:6).

I have learned to be content whatever the circumstances (Philippians 4:11).

I will give thanks to the LORD because of his righteousness; I will sing the praises of the name of the LORD Most High (Psalm 7:17).

My heart will sing your praise and not be silent
(Psalm 30:12).

I will always give thanks to God the Father for
everything, in the name of our Lord Jesus Christ
(Ephesians 5:20).

My Determination

My steering wheel shimmered with tears. Hunched over in the front seat of my car, I told God I couldn't do it anymore. I was *done*. The misery and heartache I regularly experienced in my marriage stole my joy, my appetite, and my confidence. I begged God not to make me go back.

But instead of dancing off into the sunset without a wedding ring, I did go back. Though it cost me, I went back. Through tears, I went back. Because God gently asked me if I would.

Have you been there? Are you there right now? Are you doing what God has told you to do, yet things have deteriorated to the point that you seriously doubt you can go on—and keep your sanity?

In Exodus 5:22-23 (NLT), Moses did exactly what the Lord commanded him, but things got much worse. It seemed like God didn't care. "Then Moses went back to the LORD and protested *(sound familiar?)*, 'Why have you brought all this trouble on your own people, Lord? Why did you send me? Ever since I came to Pharaoh as your spokesman *(to do what you told me!),* he has been even more brutal to your people. And you have done nothing to rescue them!'" According to Exodus 6:9, when things got harder, the people of Israel refused to listen to Moses anymore. They became discouraged by their own impatience and by their cruel bondage.

It's tempting to give up when things get hard. But that's where holy determination comes in. Holy determination means we refuse to quit, even when we're powerfully tempted to pack it in and head to Tahiti. Determination enables us to plow forward in spite of how awful things might appear, because we believe that God is able to move—that He will move—because of our determination to honor Him. When we determine to obey God, we are declaring that His plans for us supersede our own desires. Jesus, in the Garden of Gethsemane, yearned to avoid the horror of the cross, yet He was determined to yield to God's will instead of caving in to His own desires. Most of us will not be called to give up our very lives, but determination will cost us, nonetheless.

The next time you're faced with the choice to give up or to push on, ask God to help you push through. Holy determination clothes us with the strength and resolve we need to accomplish God's will and plan for our lives. It's an internal decision that boosts our ability by deciding ahead of time that we will do whatever it takes to obey the Lord.

Daily Prayer

Dear Lord,

I am in need of holy determination—the kind that strengthens my resolve and enables me to make it through hard situations. Though it will cost me, I long to be determined to live a life that pleases You in every way. Help me not to cave in to my own desires. Enable me, through determination, to say to You with a sincere heart, "Nevertheless, Your will be done" in every situation. Equip me, through godly determination inspired by You, to never give up. May my every decision reflect this holy determination.

Help me to live a determined life—determined to obey You even though it costs me, determined to please You even when it does not please my flesh, and determined to honor You through my words, thoughts, and actions.

I am determined to be determined, by Your grace. In Jesus's name, amen.

God's Word for Me

I will never tire of doing what is good
(2 Thessalonians 3:13).

I will give careful thought to the paths for my feet
and be steadfast in all my ways (Proverbs 4:26).

I will be very careful, then, how I live—not as
unwise but as wise (Ephesians 5:15).

I will not be foolish, but will understand what the
Lord's will is (Ephesians 5:17).

I want to know Christ—yes, to know the power
of his resurrection and participation in his
sufferings (Philippians 3:10).

Create in me a pure heart, O God, and renew a
steadfast spirit within me (Psalm 51:10).

I will stand firm. I will let nothing move me. I will
always give myself fully to the work of the Lord
(1 Corinthians 15:58).

My Self-Control

Occasionally I will decide to watch a TV show only to search in exasperation for the missing remote control. *Where on earth is it? Who had it last? Why can't I find it?* It usually takes no small amount of searching. I lift sofa cushions and cozy throws, check under the magazine pile on the coffee table, and then I inevitably call out "Has anyone seen the TV remote?"

I've also had days when I've wondered where on earth my *self*-control was hiding. Whether it's snarfing down yet another cookie, letting loose with a stinging retort, or allowing my body language to undeniably declare that someone has gotten on my last nerve, there's no denying my self-control has gone missing.

And speaking of remote controls, I have on occasion felt as though I was being maneuvered by some sort of emotional remote control. A friend's thoughtless comment? *Click!* Here come the tears. A thoughtless stranger's rude words at the grocery store? *Click!* Boy, am I peeved! My husband misses my cue? *Click!* My feelings are hurt!

As Christians, we have the fruit of the Holy Spirit called self-control available to us. I personally think that self-control is the last fruit listed in Galatians 5:22 because it's the most difficult fruit to produce. This particular fruit requires a lengthy ripening process, a maturing which can only occur as we abide in Jesus, spending time in His word and in prayer. Change comes as we begin to take on Christ's image.

The reason the Lord calls it self-control is because the only person in charge of this fruit is, of course, me. It's a choice. I can't blame others because I can't find my self-control. The apostle James says that if we never say the wrong things we are perfect (James 3:2), but he also admits that the human tongue can be tamed by no man (James 3:8). Thankfully, we're not left helpless, yet there is a divine paradox. Choosing to walk in self-control requires reliance on someone other than ourselves; it requires complete dependence on the Lord. Galatians 5:25 says, "Since we live by the Spirit, let us keep in step with the Spirit."

Though I cannot promise you'll never misplace the remote control for your TV again, when we choose to rely on the Lord, we'll be fully able to not only locate, but regularly use our self-control.

Daily Prayer

Father,

Your word says I can do all things through Christ who strengthens me, and that includes walking in self-control. Help me to develop self-control in every area of my life, including my emotions, my opinions, my appetite, my spending, and my habits.

Help me to walk in the Spirit so that I will not fulfill the lust of the flesh. Enable me to avoid foolish arguments by controlling my tongue, my thoughts, and my responses to those around me. I realize that self-control is my choice, but apart from You I can do nothing, so give me grace as I make the effort to grow in self-control. Help me to use self-control to establish wise, godly habits. It is through self-control that I can become more diligent, disciplined, and prudent. Thank You for enabling me to grow in this fruit of the Spirit. In Jesus's name, amen.

God's Word for Me

The Spirit produces this fruit
in my life: love, joy, peace, forbearance,
kindness, goodness, faithfulness, gentleness and
self-control. Against such things there is no law
(Galatians 5:22-23).

For the Spirit God gave me does not make me timid,
but gives me power, love, and self-discipline
(2 Timothy 1:7).

I will be diligent in exercising my faith to develop
virtue, [excellence], knowledge, and self-control
(2 Peter 1:5-6 AMP).

I can do all this through him who gives me
strength (Philippians 4:13).

I will walk by the Spirit, and I will not gratify the
desires of the flesh (Galatians 5:16).

I desire to do your will, my God; your law is
within my heart (Psalm 40:8).

I have the right to do anything, but not everything is beneficial (1 Corinthians 10:23).

My Tension-Filled Life

I don't know about you, but all of life's daily stresses always seem to settle in my neck, shoulders, and jaws, creating tight muscle knots where they clearly don't belong. And it doesn't take much for the kinks to set in. Something as simple as imagining myself eating a bowl of my favorite cereal for breakfast during my morning shower sets the stage. Later I walk into the pantry, pull out the unusually light box, and discover someone in the family ate it all—except for the tablespoon of crumbs hanging out at the bottom of the bag. Not enough to make a bowl of cereal, but enough, apparently, to leave in the box and place back on the pantry shelf. A breakfast tease. Kink one.

Then there's always the ringing telephone that no one in the house feels compelled to answer. It usually happens when I'm in the bathroom—a room without a phone, by the way. We do have phones located in four other rooms of our house, which seemingly is not enough to entice anyone into actually getting up from their comfortable positions to answer it. Before you know it, there's yet another voicemail waiting for me to listen to. Kink two.

Even good stress, like focusing intently, causes me to clench my jaws. I realized this while concentrating on directions for a Moroccan dinner recipe. And I don't think it had anything to do with the joy of using nameless, exotic spices. Kink three.

If you've noticed yourself gripping your steering wheel with a death-clench, brushing your teeth with entirely too much intensity, or scrubbing the counter with a little bit too much force, perhaps, like me, you could benefit from becoming supernaturally relaxed.

The first step in becoming a more relaxed person is simply being aware that we need to relax. This sounds obvious, but it was a huge realization for me. I had no idea that I was a walking ball of kinks. Being aware helps, but it's no cure. We need the promptings of the Holy Spirit to transform us into relaxed women of grace. So I began to pray. I asked the Lord to make me aware when I tensed up in any way. What an eye-opener! Thanks to the promptings of the Holy Spirit, I caught myself clenching my jaws no less than 15 times in a single hour. I also noticed my shoulders hunching up around my ears as I sat in front of my computer.

Because of the Holy Spirit's continuous intervention, I no longer hold my breath when I'm cleaning up a sticky spill, and my body and heart are far more relaxed and at ease. And from one former stress-ball to another, it's a far better way to live. In fact, it's literally supernatural, with awareness not only of our physical and emotional responses, but an utter dependency upon the Lord to enable us to continually walk in the Spirit—and remain supernaturally relaxed.

Daily Prayer

Heavenly Father,

I don't want to live under the physical consequences of constant stress on my body and heart, yet I realize that every life contains a measure of stress—both good and not so good stressful events. So I'm asking You to help me release and entrust every situation to Your tender care. It is not Your intention for me to walk beneath the constant load of heavy stress that creates kinks in my muscles, so I willingly relinquish every concern to You.

Please make me aware of times when stress begins affecting me—when my heart and body begin to knot up. Help me, by the power of Your Holy Spirit, to breathe deeply and choose to relax instead of allowing myself to become more and more stressed—physically, emotionally, and mentally. I desire to live as a supernaturally relaxed woman of grace, maintaining not only my composure but holding on to my peace in every situation. I can only do this by walking in the Spirit and not in the flesh so help me, Lord. Enable me to quickly respond to Your promptings and begin living a supernaturally relaxed life. In Jesus's name, amen.

God's Word for Me

I enjoy the gift of peace of mind and heart, so I will remain peaceful and not be troubled or afraid (John 14:27 NLT).

Show me your ways, LORD, teach me your paths (Psalm 25:4).

You make known to me the path of life; you will fill me with joy in your presence (Psalm 16:11).

Guide me in your truth and teach me, for you are God my Savior, and my hope is in you all day long (Psalm 25:5).

Praise be to the LORD, for he showed me the wonders of his love when I was in a city under siege (Psalm 31:21).

My heart leaps for joy, and with my song I praise him (Psalm 28:7).

I have a calm and undisturbed mind and heart. These are the life and health of my body (Proverbs 14:30 AMP).

My Comparison Issues

When I first began writing, I was overwhelmed by feelings of inferiority, mainly because I had no formal education. Every writer I came in contact with, whether at conferences, workshops, or through blogging, seemed to hold either a Bachelor's degree in journalism or a Master's degree in English literature, or something comparable. I had nothing but a G.E.D., obtained after dropping out of high school in the middle of my senior year so I could earn a living. I had moved out on my own at the age of 17 due to an unstable and unsafe home environment. This left me feeling unprepared and inadequate for life, and my struggle with comparison began.

Comparing myself to these writers made me feel intimidated and uncertain that I could or even should pursue what I felt God was nudging me toward—writing for publication. In spite of my misgivings, I moved forward, plagued by self-doubt and wishing I were as qualified as those around me.

Eventually God made it clear to me that He had trained and educated me unconventionally—His way.

I learned to stop circling the perilous ground of comparison. Whether we compare our bodies, our families, our jobs, our callings, or where we are on the journey, the temptation can be so subtle we barely recognize it. But it's dangerous ground we would be wise to avoid.

Comparing ourselves to others does a lot of things—none of them good:

It fosters insecurity. And insecure people don't get far. Insecurity prevents us from moving forward because it partners with fear to hold us back. But when we strive to know God's unique plan for our lives, we grow in both ability and confidence.

It makes us feel small. We've all experienced a moment when we felt pale and insignificant in the shadow of another. But the truth is we are exactly who God created us to be, and it grieves the Holy Spirit when we think of ourselves as less than all God's Word declares. Instead of standing in someone else's shadow and allowing ourselves to feel small, let's dwell under the shadow of the Almighty, confident in our identities and giftings as God's daughters.

It breeds competition. Comparison turns our hearts into scales—we're constantly weighing what others have against the things we lack. Remember, this is a race to the finish of our *own* God-given destiny, not a race to beat someone else. We can cheer each other on, pray for one another, and remember that we're on the same team!

It robs us of our unique identity. There's no way we can become all God intends for us to be when our eyes are on others. When we keep our focus on the Lord and His plan for us, we can grow and excel in our own individual style.

When we resist comparing ourselves to others, we become free to love and appreciate ourselves exactly as God made us. We also make it easier for God to work in and through us, and we become anchored to the One who holds our lives in His hands.

Daily Prayer

Dear Lord,

Please forgive me for comparing myself to others. Help me to resist this powerful temptation, believing that I am fearfully and wonderfully made. You created me, giving me unique talents, abilities, and personality traits that You knew I would need and could use. Please help me not to grieve You by falling into the trap of comparison.

Lord, Your word says that godliness with contentment

is great gain. Help me not to compare myself with others, but to be content with who I am, the way You created me, and the gifts You have entrusted to me. It is not Your will for me to focus on others' talents, achievements, and abilities. Help me not to focus on others, causing myself to feel insecure, small, or competitive. But instead, enable me to focus on Your plan for me and embrace my distinct identity in Christ. In Jesus's name, amen.

God's Word for Me

Keep me safe, my God, for in you I take refuge (Psalm 16:1).

Lord, you alone are my portion and my cup; you make my lot secure (Psalm 16:5).

I am one of God's chosen people (1 Peter 2:9).

His divine power has given me everything I need for a godly life through my knowledge of him (2 Peter 1:3).

I will humble myself before the Lord, and he will
lift me up and make my life significant
(James 4:10 AMP).

I trust in the LORD; I will not be shaken
(Psalm 21:7).

I will pay attention to my own work; then I will
get the satisfaction of a job well done and won't
need to compare myself to anyone else
(Galatians 6:4 NLT).

My Obedience

The old diner smelled of grease and freshly brewed coffee, an oddly comforting combination as my brother and I shook off the cold November night and slid into a booth. We rarely got time alone to talk, what with him stationed at a naval base in Virginia and me living hundreds of miles away in Florida.

As he added sugar to his coffee and I sipped my hot chocolate, our conversation wrapped around one thing—my new relationship with Jesus. Giddy and convinced I'd go to the ends of the earth for my God, I declared I'd do anything—anything at all for Him.

Looking John in the eyes, I leaned forward. "I'd even go to China if He wanted me to!" At the time, China seemed like the last place I'd ever want to be, so I tossed my daring declaration into the air like so much sparkling confetti. Part of me hoped God wouldn't take me up on it, but if He did, I'd go. I'd certainly go.

"Wow, Julie." John sipped his coffee. "Maybe God *will* send you to China."

I positively glowed.

But over 20 years later, it turns out that God didn't want me to go to China. Or India. Or Africa. Instead, He asked me to do something even more radical.

He asked me to stay.

God asked me to stay in an ugly marriage when everything in me wanted to run fast and hard. He asked me to remain a homeschooling mom while kids all around us waltzed off to school and I craved a quiet, tidy home—and time for me. He asked me to remain a loving mother-in-law even when that love wasn't initially returned. He asked me to stay committed to prayer when I didn't see the results for which I yearned. Today God continues to ask us to forgive when we want to hold a grudge, remain kind with our words when we long to scream out in retaliation, and stay true to our course when we'd like to flat-out quit.

First John 1:6 says "If we claim to have fellowship with him and yet walk in the darkness, we lie and do not live out the truth." Jesus was obedient even to the point of death. While few of us will be asked to literally die, we will probably be asked to do something that our flesh would rather not do. In John 14:15 Jesus declares, "If you love me, keep my commands." Our obedience to God won't necessarily require us to go to the ends of the earth. But if we're willing, it will probably cost us more than we ever imagined.

Daily Prayer

Heavenly Father,

Though my heart longs to be obedient to You, I confess it's sometimes far easier to think about obeying You than actually doing it. And if I'm honest, there are plenty of times I'd rather do things my way. So Lord, please grant me a willing heart to sustain me. Give me the grace to obey You even when it's difficult, awkward, or inconvenient.

Help me to honor You with my choices, and help me to choose to please You and bring You glory through obedience even when it costs me. I realize obedience will sometimes make things harder for me initially, but in the long run it's far better to endure hard times and remain in the center of Your will than to have my own way in ease apart from You. Lord, I understand that obedience is something I need to learn and grow in, and right now I make the decision to willingly obey You. Thank You for empowering me by Your Holy Spirit. In Jesus's name, amen.

God's Word for Me

Restore to me the joy of your salvation and grant
me a willing spirit, to sustain me (Psalm 51:12).

I face death every day—yes, just as surely as I
boast about you in Christ Jesus our Lord
(1 Corinthians 15:31).

Does the LORD delight in burnt offerings and
sacrifices as much as obeying the LORD?
(1 Samuel 15:22).

As an obedient child, I will not conform to the
evil desires I had when I lived in ignorance
(1 Peter 1:14).

If I love God truly [with affectionate reverence
and prompt obedience] I am known by God
(1 Corinthians 8:3 AMP).

All Scripture is God-breathed (2 Timothy 3:16).

I will love others deeply, from the heart
(1 Peter 1:22).

My Desire to Be Noticed

My reaction startled even me. Tears threatening, I stood in the hallway during the middle of a busy conference and tried to get a grip. It wasn't working. Through no one's intention, my name had been left off of a valued piece of writing work, and I felt crushed. Worse, I couldn't understand my strong response to this discovery. Sure, it would have been nice to have my name listed on the credits. But stuff happens, and I assumed it was unintentional. So why was I feeling so upset?

I decided to get back to my room so I could pray and hear from the Lord about what was going on inside my heart. Though I didn't receive an immediate answer, I did receive Jesus's overwhelming peace and went on to enjoy the rest of the conference. It wasn't until a few weeks later, when my schedule settled down and I was finally home from additional traveling, that I had time alone with God to really pour out my heart, and more importantly, listen. Though I sensed God was at work, I still didn't have an answer.

Then one afternoon, I phoned a cherished close friend and shared the scenario with her. To my relief, God spoke. Angela's words were loving but to the point. "What I'm hearing is a little girl who has worked really hard, and has run to show her mommy her work and get her approval, but her mommy didn't notice or care. Does that make sense?"

It did, if my fresh tears and the accompanying hallelujah chorus were any indication. Though I felt relieved to know the root of my feelings, I felt stunned that apparently, deep down, I still had the capacity to feel like an overlooked little girl. But God knew. And He allowed the oversight to happen to bring this issue to the surface of my heart so He could dislodge that root and bring healing and wholeness to my heart.

Although our childhood, life's disappointments, or painful situations may leave our hearts feeling overlooked, Jehovah El-Roi is the One who sees. He notices us, lavishes His attention on us, and is delighted to look at whatever we bring to Him.

When deep down we long to be noticed, we can remember there is One who always notices us. He encourages us to run to Him with our achievements, our concerns, and our hurts. Because God is the One who sees, we can share the most private, intimate portions of our inner selves with Him, because He sees what's there, and He understands our needs—needs that only He can truly satisfy.

God always sees our efforts and hard work, and our thirsty souls can drink in His loving concern, approval, and encouragement. We never have to feel overlooked again! Because the truth is, we're not. Our heavenly Father is truly the God who sees.

Daily Prayer

Dear Lord,

I'm so grateful that You are the God who sees. You see me, my heart, and my achievements, and You always notice my efforts. Thank You, God, for dislodging the roots in my life that have caused me to feel overlooked. Lord, heal my heart and my emotions from childhood events, disappointments, and situations that led to my feeling overlooked. I realize that no one can ultimately fill my need for being noticed except You.

When I'm tempted to feel overlooked, Lord, help me to remember that You are the God who sees. You are always available and joyfully, eagerly ready to notice me and the work, events, and situations I'm involved in. Thank You, Father, for paying attention to me even when I don't realize it. You are always there for me! I will receive my desire for being noticed from You and You alone because You are the God who sees me. In Jesus's name, amen.

God's Word for Me

You have searched me, LORD, and you know me (Psalm 139:1).

I pour out my complaint; before Him I tell my trouble (Psalm 142:2).

In my distress I called to the LORD; I cried to my God for help. From his temple he heard my voice; my cry came before him, into his ears (Psalm 18:6).

Though the mountains be shaken and the hills be removed, the LORD's unfailing love for me will not be shaken (Isaiah 54:10).

You encourage me, and you listen to my cry (Psalm 10:17).

The LORD watches over the way of the righteous
(Psalm 1:6).

Yet the LORD longs to be gracious to me; therefore
he will rise up to show me compassion
(Isaiah 30:18).

My Patience

My Christian walk is never tested more than when I'm driving. A classic Type A personality, I like to get from here to there as quickly and efficiently as possible. So, cruising behind a car traveling 10 miles per hour *below* the speed limit on a two-lane road that stretches for ten miles is not only a cruel test of my patience (or the noticeable lack thereof), it's a recipe for making steam escape from my ears in wild plumes.

And apparently I'm not the only one. During the month of December, my husband and I snuck out of the house early one Saturday morning to beat the crowds and accomplish some Christmas shopping. As we cruised through a shopping center parking lot, the dude behind us in a black Mercedes convertible laid on the horn, indicating that my hubby was driving too slowly. It didn't seem to concern this less than happy driver that we were in a busy parking lot. He wanted us to go faster—right now.

My husband simply ignored him and continued driving safely toward our destination. When Keith turned left and began rolling into a parking space, the Mercedes man squealed in from the other side and our cars nearly collided. In a rage, the guy proceeded to curse us and then stormed off to a nearby store. I was stunned. But then my heart did a drastic pause, and as the day went on I got honest with myself. Apart from the cussing and dangerous aggression, how was I any different than this guy? I loathed driving behind slow drivers, too, and frequently lamented the traffic situation on any given day, with my daughter in the car, no less. Was my impatience while driving an indication of my need to grow in this area? And what about other situations?

As I thought about it, I began to realize that I demonstrated impatience multiple times on any given day—and not only in my car. And I felt challenged to make a concerted effort, with God's grace, to grow from a fuming, impatient woman to one from whom steam rarely escapes.

Whether you fume in traffic or feel impatient at the status of a relationship, your job, or where your life is in general, the truth is our impatience holds the potential to hurt others and grieve the Holy Spirit. Though we can't kid ourselves into thinking that patience blossoms instantly, we can choose to make the commitment to grow in patience. This involves learning to trust God and His timing with all things in our lives, including how soon we get from here to there. Romans 15:5 says "May the God who gives endurance and encouragement give you the same attitude of mind toward each other that Christ Jesus had." As we begin to pray this week, we can patiently trust the Lord and cooperate with the promptings of the Holy Spirit. Then we absolutely can begin to live in authentic patience.

Daily Prayer

Dear Lord,

Forgive me for the many times I've demonstrated impatience and allowed it to sway my behavior. I don't want to exhibit all the fallout of impatience: complaining, whining, exasperation, aggravation, and an all-around lack of peace. Instead, I long to be grateful, speak words of grace, and walk in patience to honor You. If love is patient, then clearly I need more of Your love at work within me. Fill and flood my heart with Your love so that I am a body wholly filled with You, God. When I sense the steam of impatience beginning to billow, enable me to take a deep, calming breath of Your unfailing love instead. Help me to rejoice in hope and be patient in suffering. Help me to trust Your timing in every area of my life. I lift up my relationships and the changes I long to see, the dreams I long to see fulfilled, the situations I'm facing, and my own personality and ask You to move in every one of them. Help me to learn to grow in patience. Thank You for the patient endurance that comes from Christ alone. Keep my heart consistently peaceful, calm, and patient in Christ Jesus. Amen.

God's Word for Me

It's better for me to be patient than powerful;
to have self-control than to conquer a city
(Proverbs 16:32 NLT).

I will be still before the LORD and wait patiently
for him (Psalm 37:7).

I will wait for the LORD; I will be strong and take
heart and wait for the LORD (Psalm 27:14).

May the Lord direct my heart into God's love and
Christ's perseverance (2 Thessalonians 3:5).

I will be completely humble and gentle
(Ephesians 4:2).

I need to persevere so that when I have done the
will of God, I will receive what he has promised
(Hebrews 10:36).

I will patiently endure testing and temptation
and receive the crown of life
(James 1:12 NLT).

My Trust in God

S he lay in the hospital crib as limp as an old dish towel, too weak to even whimper. My sweet baby girl, burning up with fever, received precious fluids from the IV pumping into her vein. Morning and night she had vomited uncontrollably as a raging stomach virus ran its course. But the inability to retain fluids of any kind, along with the fever, had turned from a serious nuisance to a serious concern in just two days. When I took her to the pediatrician that afternoon, the doctor didn't hesitate to admit my three-year-old daughter into the hospital.

After spending the first 48 hours by Emily's side, sleep deprivation gave me a wild-eyed look that startled even the most experienced nurses. That evening my husband, Keith, insisted on staying overnight with our daughter so I could go home to shower and get a good night's sleep in my own bed. In the meantime, our nine-year-old son was in good hands with Keith's mom.

When I arrived home that evening, I was tempted to throw myself onto our bed and sob—and who would have blamed me? I was exhausted, smelled awful, and my baby girl still couldn't hold down even a teaspoon of water. This was her fourth hospitalization for a serious stomach virus in the past two years; I was fed up, and emotionally and spiritually exhausted. I couldn't understand why God was allowing this to happen, and I truly struggled to trust Him with my treasured baby girl.

Yet as the spray of hot water hit the tiled shower floor that night, a holy indignation took hold of me. I realized I didn't have time for self-pity or doubt. As I lathered, I began to do the only thing I could think of to show the enemy what I thought of his evil schemes against my daughter. I began to sing. I sang every worship song I could think of, and in between each one, I declared aloud that I trusted the Lord.

When we're facing situations that make us wonder what God is doing and why He hasn't intervened, what we're really wondering is whether or not we can trust Him. And while it isn't always easy, it is possible to trust the Lord regardless of how things appear. When circumstances look scary, unsettling, or grim, we can face reality while truly trusting that God is not only in control, but that He will have the final say in our situations. While there are no guarantees this side of heaven, we can choose to truly trust the One who holds our times in His hands. Because the truth is, God is faithful and utterly trustworthy.

Daily Prayer

Dear Lord,

I long to genuinely trust You in every area of my life and in every situation that unfolds, regardless of how things appear. I want to say, like the psalmist, that when I am afraid I will trust in You. I want to know, like Peter, that if You tell me to walk on the water, I can trust You to enable me. I want to agree with You, like Mary, who trusted You and declared "Let it be done unto me as You have said." When circumstances tempt me to doubt that You are trustworthy, help me to remember that You are faithful and true. You have plans for my good and not for my harm, plans to prosper me and to give me hope and a future.

While I don't always understand what is happening, Lord, my heart can rest at ease in Your presence as I release every area of my life to You, trusting that You will cause all things to work for my good, because I love You and I'm called according to Your purpose. Help me to continually trust You, Father. You alone are worthy of my trust, and I choose now to trust You. In Jesus's name, amen.

God's Word for Me

In peace I will lie down and sleep, for you alone, LORD, make me dwell in safety (Psalm 4:8).

I will take refuge in you and be glad; I will ever sing for joy. Spread your protection over me, that I may rejoice in you (Psalm 5:11).

Those who know your name trust in you, for you, LORD, have never forsaken those who seek you (Psalm 9:10).

The Lord is my rock, my fortress and my deliverer; my God is my rock, in whom I take refuge (Psalm 18:2).

The LORD shields me as I take refuge in him (Psalm 18:30).

Keep me safe, my God, for in you I take refuge, and in you do I put my trust (Psalm 16:1).

When I am afraid, I will put my trust in you (Psalm 56:3).

My Confidence

We walked onto the movie set of "Flipped," a Rob Reiner film set in the early 1960s, feeling nervous and excited. This Warner Brothers picture would be my then 14-year-old daughter's first experience as an extra. Our first stop was wardrobe, where Emily was fitted into a cute robin's-egg-blue dress with a white Peter Pan collar and black flats.

As I watched my daughter interact with the hair and wardrobe people and then talk to the assistant director, I marveled at her confidence. All throughout her two weeks on the set, she laughed and played games with the other extras while they waited for shooting to begin, shook hands with the stars of the movie, and interacted with the professionals with ease. She took direction well and proved herself to be capable and self-assured. Frankly, she seemed more sure of herself than I ever did at her age, and I thanked God for it.

I fought serious intimidation, insecurity, and uncertainty from a young age, and those issues continued to plague me into adulthood, leaving me with little confidence. Until I met Jesus. Now I don't want to mislead you into thinking I gave my heart and life to the Lord and then *poof!* all of those concerns evaporated. But as I studied God's word and grew in my understanding of Jesus's power and ability to transform even the most unlikely people, the bonds around my heart and mind began to loosen. Little by little, my confidence began to grow.

When we long to grow in confidence, we need to realize that our heavenly Father is not only able to replace our doubts and fears, but that He yearns to fill us with His supernatural confidence. This confidence is a transformational work of the Holy Spirit that can only be accomplished through a steady, authentic, ever-increasing relationship with Jesus.

As we grow in our knowledge, belief, and acceptance of who we are in Christ, our old ways of thinking and feeling genuinely change. Intimidation is replaced by courage. Insecurity is swapped for unfathomable security in Christ. And uncertainty is exchanged for a deep confidence that cannot be shaken.

This confidence that the Lord gives us is not arrogant, self-important, or dismissive. It's a holy confidence deep in our souls—the result of the deep, ongoing work of the Holy Spirit. It enables us to assertively meet the tasks, opportunities, and relationships He places into our lives with utter confidence in Jesus. As Philippians 4:13 says, "I can do all this through him who gives me strength." As we pray about our confidence this week, let's focus on the fact that God can fill us with His holy confidence.

Daily Prayer

Dear Heavenly Father,

I long to experience the authentic confidence that only You provide. Please replace any intimidation in my heart with courage. Enable me to be strong and courageous. Swap out any insecurity within my heart for the unfathomable security found in Christ. And exchange the uncertainty I feel with a deep confidence in You that cannot be shaken. Because Your word says to put no confidence in the flesh, I realize that my confidence cannot lie in my own ability, Lord, but needs to come completely from You. Help me to grow closer to You, knowing with full confidence that if I draw near to You, Lord, You will draw near to me.

Thank You for filling me with godly confidence. Thank You for enabling me to possess a strong and confident heart. And thank You for Your grace actively at work in my life, enabling me to grow in wisdom and stature, and in grace, truth, and confidence. In Jesus's mighty name, amen.

God's Word for Me

Have mercy on me, my God, have mercy on me, for in you I take refuge. I will take refuge in the shadow of your wings until the disaster has passed (Psalm 57:1).

I will trust in him at all time; I will pour out my heart to him, for God is my refuge (Psalm 62:8).

For you have been my hope, Sovereign Lord, my confidence since my youth (Psalm 71:5).

For the Lord will be at my side and will keep my foot from being snared (Proverbs 3:26).

When I am afraid, I will have confidence and put my trust and reliance in You (Psalm 56:3 AMP).

You, my God, have revealed to me that you will build a house for me. So I have found courage to pray to you (1 Chronicles 17:25).

I have the reverent and worshipful fear of the Lord and strong confidence, and I shall always have a place of refuge (Proverbs 14:26 AMP).

My Perfectionism

It was only a bag of chips falling to the kitchen pantry floor, so my angry response puzzled me. I didn't understand why I berated myself with my own words, and why small annoyances always felt like such a huge deal to me. My livid reaction was completely disproportionate and once I had calmed down, I was left wondering why similar scenarios continued to happen in spite of my best efforts.

Then one morning I sensed the Holy Spirit impressing His insight into my heart. As I stopped and listened, I began to understand that throughout my life, I had demanded nothing less than 100 percent perfection from myself at all times, and anything less triggered an irrational response.

The major reason for this response was that as a girl, I became fearful of my dad's explosive temper. I determined to avoid his belt by doing everything right and being ultra-careful in everything I said and did. Of course this put immense pressure on me, creating an unhealthy, unrealistic expectation for perfectionism.

Little did I realize that as I grew up, the inner pressure for perfectionism I had created never disappeared.

As an adult, that pressure roared to life when I made the slightest mistake. It served as an invisible mooring which prevented me from moving forward despite my best efforts. No screaming parent towered over me—instead, I had taken on the role of berating myself over silly mistakes.

My jaw dropped as I pondered all this. Then I sensed God's gentle whisper to my heart. *You don't have to be perfect, Julie. I am perfect for you. And I am releasing you from the dread and perfectionism that holds you back.*

Lofty standards and a desire to always get it right may seem like noble goals, but they only set us up for intense pressure, frustration, and disappointment. It's not that we shouldn't strive for excellence, but we need to understand the difference between pursuing excellence and pursuing perfection. True excellence is simply doing our very best—perfectionism demands a flawless performance at all times.

Whether our perfectionist tendencies are rooted in fear, striving, control, or pride, God wants us to know that perfection was only required once, and Jesus met that standard. It is through Jesus's blood and the finished work of the cross that we are released from the pressure-inducing goal of self-perfection. We are then freed to radically pursue true perfection: our heavenly Father.

Daily Prayer

Heavenly Father,

I want to be free of the desire for perfectionism. I realize that only one perfect person ever lived—Jesus—and that He accomplished for me what I am unable to do myself. Please help me to break this cycle of striving toward the impossible. I long to experience freedom from the pressures I place on myself and others in trying to attain unrealistic goals of self-perfection. Help me not to demand perfection from myself or from others. I long to rest in the finished work of the cross, trusting that Jesus's blood covers my mistakes.

Whatever the root cause of any unhealthy striving toward personal self-perfection, I ask You to bring freedom and release me in the name of Jesus. Help me to cooperate with You in the days and weeks ahead so I can grow in Christ's freedom. This is not an excuse to wallow in laziness or ignore my responsibilities. By Your grace, I will continue to do my best and pursue excellence, but only as You lead and enable me, and for Your honor and glory. Thank You for freedom from perfectionism, Lord! In Jesus's name, amen.

God's Word for Me

For your name's sake, LORD, preserve my life; in your righteousness, bring me out of trouble (Psalm 143:11).

It is for freedom that Christ has set me free. I will stand firm, then, and will not let myself be burdened again by a yoke of slavery (Galatians 5:1).

Now the Lord is the Spirit, and where the Spirit of the Lord is, there is freedom (2 Corinthians 3:17).

Grace and peace is mine in abundance through the knowledge of God and of Jesus our Lord (2 Peter 1:2).

I will not be foolish after starting my life in the Spirit, by trying to become perfect by my own human effort (Galatians 3:3 NLT).

When hard pressed, I cried to the LORD; he brought me into a spacious place (Psalm 118:5).

The LORD is God, and he has made his light shine on me (Psalm 118:27).

My Marriage

My marriage felt like happily never after. A torturous honeymoon during which wedding rings were flung onto the rental car dashboard was our entrance into years of harsh words and accumulated hurts. It was definitely not what I signed up for.

Two years later I became a believer and was convinced God would promptly intervene and change my husband—and bring peace, happiness, and a sweeping dose of romantic love to my miserable marriage.

But in spite of my prayers God didn't instantaneously transform my husband from a beast to a prince—He was far more interested in transforming *me* into the image of His beauty. My journey toward a healthy marriage began with the simple, obedient step of praying. For me. In that process, I was utterly undone. My mind, attitude, lurking unforgiveness, and years of hurts corroding the chambers of my heart were pinpointed with laser focus by the Holy Spirit.

As God used my prayers to heal and transform *me*, the most amazing shift unfolded in my marriage.

Subtly, almost imperceptibly at first, came a gradual thaw. To my amazement, buds began springing out of what had been parched ground. Yes, love finally blossomed in my marriage. All the promises I had sensed God whispering to my heart over all those hard years began to emerge, one tender blade at a time.

A close friend really helped me at this point. She objectively observed and perceived specific, good changes and encouraged me by pointing them out. Because of that, I adjusted my prayers. *God, help me to see the small, incremental changes. Help me to continue to trust You when we have setbacks. Help my husband and me to love and enjoy You, and love and enjoy each other.* Because the truth is, change is hardly ever instantaneous. It's more of a holy process. Especially in marriage.

Now instead of a consistently bad marriage with an occasional reprieve of happy moments, I have a good marriage with occasional arguments. Sometimes those arguments are minute and sometimes they teeter on the gargantuan. But now we have the hearts and tools to resolve our issues—with God's help.

The amazing part is that we're now on the brink of celebrating our 26th wedding anniversary. We communicate fairly well (I mean, we *are* still a man and a woman…), we've learned to laugh at ourselves—a vital component in every marriage—and we also pray together nightly before bed. God has accomplished the seemingly impossible, because ultimately, nothing is too difficult for Him.

Daily Prayer

Dear Lord,

You alone know the hurts, the disappointments, the anger, and the loneliness I've faced at times during my marriage. Help me to forgive my husband, and please bring healing to the areas of my heart that have been wounded. I realize this is a process, but I desire to cooperate with You and will trust and obey You every step of the way.

God, where love has died, resurrect it. Cause our love for You and for one another to increase. Grant me godly perspective. I pray that mercy will flourish in my relationship with my spouse. Help me not to judge, disrespect, or dishonor my husband. Help me to speak positive, encouraging words to him. Enable me to perceive and recognize specific, good changes as You work . Enable my husband and me to enjoy You

and enjoy each other. Fill us with Your joy and grant us
grace for the hard moments. Help us to extend grace
to each other and always think the best of each other.
Bring godly transformation in our hearts and our lives
in Jesus's mighty name, amen.

God's Word for Me

And now these three remain: faith, hope and love.
But the greatest of these is love
(1 Corinthians 13:13).

I will be joyful, grow to maturity, encourage
others, and live in harmony and peace
(2 Corinthians 13:11 NLT).

Your grace is sufficient for me, for your power is
made perfect in weakness (2 Corinthians 12:9).

My husband and I will bear with each other and
forgive each other if either us has a grievance
against the other. We will forgive as the Lord
forgave us (Colossians 3:13).

I will submit myself to my own husband as I do
to the Lord (Ephesians 5:22).

I will respect my husband, [notice him, regard
him, honor him, praise him, and love and
admire him exceedingly]
(Ephesians 5:33 AMP).

Whatever happens, I will conduct myself in a
manner worthy of the gospel of Christ.
My husband and I will stand firm in the one
Spirit, striving together as one for the faith
of the gospel (Philippians 1:27).

My Calling

I wrote a lot of books between the ages of 9 and 11, and they all had one thing in common: a hand-colored front page (usually featuring a dilapidated old house) with three precisely placed staples. But then my family life took an ugly turn, and the joy of writing was buried.

My dream to write only resurfaced after many years in an intimate, personal relationship with Jesus. God began to reveal to me (through literal dreams, no less!) that I had buried the gift of communication He had entrusted to me. By that time, I was approaching the age of 40 and stunned about these revelations. The gift of writing was so deeply buried I did not even remember it existed. Oddly, I did not connect the joyful passions of a little girl to the calling God had on my life.

So how did a nearly 40-year-old woman shift gears and begin to finally reclaim and then pursue the dream God gave her? For me, it was a process—sort of like a slow awakening. If you come from a difficult background, know this: It's never too late and you're not

239

too damaged to pursue your God-given dreams. Below are five keys to help you know your calling:

1. **Ask God to reveal any talents that are buried.** Few of us get through life unscathed. Physical and emotional wounds take their tolls in different ways, but I believe that the enemy of our souls uses hurts to prevent us from fulfilling our God-given destinies. Ask God if you've been sidetracked. Implore Him to clearly show you His purpose for your life. Ask for confirmation, wisdom, and clear direction.

2. **Recognize and articulate the dream.** This was a hard one for me, because my dreams were submerged beneath a lot of dirt. But Jesus stooped down, unearthed my dream, brushed it off, and graciously handed it back to me. This required a lot of prayerful listening on my part, a willingness to allow Him to restore the passion for a long-lost destiny, and then time for my focus to become sharp and clear. Habakkuk 2:2 says "Write down the revelation and make it plain on tablets so that a herald may run with it."

3. **Ask God to bring healing.** We're all works in progress, but in order for us to effectively minister in any capacity we need His healing touch in our

hearts, our emotions, and our lives. No, God does not require perfection before we step out. And yes, our testimonies are powerful. But we want to be careful to minister out of His love, not out of our hurt.

4. **Dare to believe what God shows you.** Initially I thought, "You must be kidding!" I didn't want my name *out there* and resisted my "public" calling because of fear and lack of education. I felt totally unqualified. But God wants us to believe Him. God "selected (deliberately chose) what in the world is foolish to put the wise to shame, and what the world calls weak to put the strong to shame" (1 Corinthians 1:27 AMP).

5. **Run with it.** Dreams are where faith, passion, and hard work collide. When we diligently apply ourselves and cooperate with the Holy Spirit, our dreams begin to unfold. Yes, we start out taking baby steps. But eventually we will run like the wind—empowered by God's grace.

Daily Prayer

Dear Lord,

You are the giver of every good and perfect gift, and I believe that includes the gifts and talents You desire for me to use to bless others and bring You glory. Please show me if I have gotten sidetracked in life and buried any talents that You've entrusted to me. Help me to understand and recognize what You reveal to my heart. Bring clarity, wisdom, and direction as I continue to seek Your direction.

In Your perfect timing, help me to know specifically all that you've called me to. Help me to believe and trust You as Your plan and purpose for my life begins to unfold. Give me boldness, joy, and confidence as I pursue Your will, targeting more accurately Your assignments and plans for me. Enable me to move forward in Your grace and assurance, knowing with confidence that You order my steps and confirm my way. Thank You, Father, for the gift of hearing Your voice and knowing the callings You have on my life. In Jesus's wonderful name, amen.

God's Word for Me

I consider my life worth nothing to me; my only aim is to finish the race and complete the task the Lord Jesus has given me (Acts 20:24).

I press on toward the goal to win the prize for which God has called me heavenward in Christ Jesus (Philippians 3:14).

My mouth will speak words of wisdom; the meditation of my heart will give you understanding (Psalm 49:3).

Give me understanding, so that I may keep your law and obey it with all my heart (Psalm 119:34).

I follow the precepts of the LORD; I have good understanding (Psalm 111:10).

I will trust in the LORD with all my heart and lean not on my own understanding (Proverbs 3:5).

Discretion will protect me, and understanding will guard me (Proverbs 2:11).

My Love for Scripture

For years I slept with a Bible under my pillow, because my aunt told me she did, and that I should too. So at night I always made sure that our small household Bible was securely under my pillow, believing that it somehow made a difference. My aunt said that sleeping with a Bible under my pillow would ensure good dreams, make me feel safe, and protect me. Funny thing is, it never did. That's because the Bible isn't meant to be stuffed beneath a pillow, but to be poured into our hearts and minds.

I know people who own a Bible but never remove it from the dusty shelf it sits on, let alone open its pages and absorb the truths within. Like the Bible hidden beneath my pillow night after night, unread Scripture does absolutely no good to anyone. The truth is, there are no shortcuts to retrieving the wisdom, comfort, and encouragement available in Scripture. If we wish to be strong in spirit and grow in wisdom and grace, then it's imperative that we cultivate a love for God's word.

One of the ways we can cultivate a love for Scripture is to recognize our desperate need for the transformational truths it contains. Like a seatbelt in a fast-moving car, God's Word acts as a restraint in our lives, buckling us securely in its wisdom and preventing us from unnecessary injury in life's fender-benders and accidents.

Maintaining a regular Bible-reading time is a non-negotiable priority that fortifies us like a satisfying meal. Most of us would never dream of consistently skipping dinner, the main meal of the day. Yet when we neglect time in God's word, we neglect the hearty fortification it offers and leave ourselves spiritually depleted, weak, and so hungry we'll be tempted to consume other things in its place. When we make time to regularly read our Bibles, we're actually making time to honor God, get to know Him intimately, transform our minds, flood our souls with peace, and discover the answers to many of our daily dilemmas.

The Bible is filled with much more than wise words—it contains truth and life, and reveals the character and lovingkindness of its Author. The very words we read are living and active, sharper than any two-edged sword (Hebrews 4:12); they are God-breathed and profitable for instruction (2 Timothy 3:16); they act as a mirror, reflecting the truth of our souls and transforming us into God's very own image (2 Corinthians 3:18). Ultimately, the key to cultivating a love for God's Word is understanding its value and power. Scripture is a priceless treasure that the wise woman stores up in her heart; she willingly and eagerly commits to absorbing, cherishing, and developing a respect and love for God's word.

Daily Prayer

Dear Lord,

Help me to realize my desperate need for the regular intake of Scripture. Because Your Word is living and active, it can penetrate my heart, my mind, and my soul, and bring about godly transformation I long for. As I read Your Word more and more, I will more accurately reflect Your image and become more like You, Lord. Enable me to value and cherish Scripture as the holy, precious treasure that it is. I long for my treasure to be You and Your Word. I will regularly hide Your Word in my heart and not sin against You.

Help me to embrace the self-discipline and diligence required to habitually read Scripture. When

distractions come, help me to remain focused
and conscientious and always make time for quiet
moments absorbing, meditating, and reflecting on
Your word. Thank You for granting me the grace not
to grow weary in doing good as I purpose to give
Scripture the place in my life and heart it deserves. In
Jesus's wonderful name, amen.

God's Word for Me

I have hidden your word in my heart that I might
not sin against you (Psalm 119:11).

God's word will not return to him empty, but will
accomplish what he desires and achieve the purpose for which he sent it (Isaiah 55:11).

For the word of God is alive and active. Sharper
than any double-edged sword, it judges the
thoughts and attitudes of the heart
(Hebrews 4:12).

All Scripture is God-breathed and is useful for
teaching, rebuking, correcting and training in
righteousness (2 Timothy 3:16).

I am being transformed into his image with ever-increasing glory, which comes from the Lord, who is the Spirit (2 Corinthians 3:18).

When I walk, God's word will guide me; when I sleep, it will watch over me; when I awake, it will speak to me (Proverbs 6:21-22).

My God-Given Destiny

I'd never done anything so frightening in my life. Attending my first writers' conference gave me shaky hands and wobbling knees, and by the second day I was a basket case. I couldn't even manage to eat, unless you count occasional sips of Nesquik chocolate milk. In fact, I was so overwhelmed I nearly left the conference early. During the lunch break on that second day, I huddled in my van, cracked open my cell phone to call my husband, and told him I couldn't go through with it all and wanted to come home.

"You don't understand!" I whimpered. "I have no idea what I'm doing!"

He laughed in a sympathetic sort of way. "And that's exactly why you need to go in there and learn."

Our conversation continued with me venting a multitude of fears and insecurities, and my husband calmly explaining that this was the very beginning of all I'd dreamed of doing for years. Finally his assurances penetrated my heart. "You can do this," he whispered. God used Keith's words and my desire to be obedient to propel me beyond my doubts and fears.

I took a deep breath, stepped out of my van, brushed the tissue lint off of my black pants, and walked back into the conference—that much closer to my God-given destiny.

I believe that each one of us has a God-given destiny. In fact, Ephesians 2:10 says that "For we are God's handiwork, created in Christ Jesus to do good works, which God prepared in advance for us to do." This exciting verse reveals that God has orchestrated opportunities for us—that they're ready and waiting for us. Our part isn't always easy: We must obey, work hard, overcome our fears, and walk in those prearranged paths. But equipped by Christ we can do it.

For some of us, fulfilling our God-given destinies will probably be the hardest thing we ever do. But it will also be the most rewarding, satisfying part of our lives. As we determine to fulfill God's plans and purposes for our lives, our faith will stretch and our understanding of God's sovereignty will increase. But most of all, our lives will be a living testimony to God's goodness and His power, and He will be glorified in and through us. Whatever your age, whatever your gifting, and whatever your dreams, know this: It's not too late, your gift is valuable, and fulfilling your God-given destiny is possible.

Daily Prayer

Dear Lord,

I believe You have a reason for me to be on this earth, and that there are specific tasks You have ordained ahead of time for me to fulfill. I sincerely long to accomplish all that You have for me to do in my life-time. Please grant me a persevering, willing, and bold heart, and equip and enable me through the power of Your Holy Spirit to fulfill the destiny You have for me. Cause my thoughts to become agreeable to Your will, and then my plans will be established and succeed. Help me to do my part by cooperating with You, working hard, and persisting in determination even when things become difficult.

Open the doors You want opened for me, and close the doors You want closed for me. Grant me divine connections, divine opportunities, divine relationships, and divine friendships. Strengthen me, order my steps, and help me to use my time on this earth well. I want to hear You say, "Well done, good and faithful servant" when we meet face to face. In Jesus's name, amen.

God's Word for Me

I consider my life worth nothing to me; my only aim is to finish the race and complete the task the Lord Jesus has given me (Acts 20:24).

Many plans are in my heart, but it is the Lord's purpose that prevails (Proverbs 19:21).

There is surely a future hope for me, and my hope will not be cut off (Proverbs 23:18).

The Lord knows the plans he has for me—plans to prosper me and not to harm me, plans to give me a hope and a future (Jeremiah 29:11).

He is before all things, and in him all things hold together (Colossians 1:17).

He who began a good work in me will carry it on to completion (Philippians 1:6).

May he give me the desires of my heart and make all my plans succeed (Psalm 20:4).